GLOSSARY OF MILITARY ABBREVIATIONS

GLOSSARY OF MILITARY ABBREVIATIONS

By
K. K SINGH
M. Sc. (Mathematics),
PGDBM (HR/Marketing)
C.A.- IIB, an Ex-Serviceman, Banker and HR/ Administration/Facilities/IR -Professional.

Neha Publishers & Distributors
4832/24, Prahlad Lane, S-207 Ansari Raod, Daryaganj, New Delhi-110002

Published by
Neha Publishers & Distributors
4832/24, Prahlad Lane, S-207 Ansari Raod, Daryaganj,
New Delhi-110002
Tel.: 011-43570976, 23278261
Email-nehapubdistributors@gmail.com

First Edition : 2013

ISBN : 978-93-80318-47-9

Price : 425/-

Laser Typesetting by : Vinod Bhardwaj

Printed at: VIKAS COMPUTERS,Delhi

PRINTED IN INDIA

Published by Neha Publishers & Distributors, New Delhi-110002

PREFACE

This book has been designed to meet the requirements of all the People of India or abroad who are interested in History , Geography, Psychology and effects of Science and Technologies on the Indo-China War and Indo-China Relations in past and effects of that war in the present and future. Students who are preparing for different Competitions with regard to Army Navy and Air Force and for the onward studies of Courses at different Arny Colleges and Scools or taking lessons at the august Universities of India or abroad. It would be helpful for all who are appearing at graduation or post graduation in the Army, Navy and Air Force in the the Indian Universities. This type of knowledge must be known to ALL.

This book is not only limited to Battle Field but also have numerous amount of knowledgeable informations and rational activities. Every educated person has write to know the all round knowledge of the world.

The present book is a novel attempt to cover a wide range of the problems of societies. This book faces very busy ideological preparedness in my life. I have written about different knowledgeable matters though it is not our area of professional work., it is in the context of all round subjects that we have studied partially , but in this book it has by no means unlimited to that context.

The problem is not a lack of knowledge or resources. The real problem is that they simply do not read those things. They spend their time spinning their wheels, attending meetings and responding to every little query and p.oblem.

And to so many others who have been left unnamed. We are also grateful to the United States of America and United Kingdom of England for their great help from Educational Associations of Literature Studies, which provided a literature, without that nothing was possible. I am also thankful to community of colleagues whose help and advice improved the quality of our thinking and portrayal of this book.

What I have described in this book are as follows:

- Film and Craft,
- Health and Wellness,
- Mental Development and Wonderful thoughts,
- History and Government,
- Science and Technology
- Law and Order- Policing,
- Internet and computer

(Total 108 topics)

This book seeks to serve as a reliable guide and companion to all students and educated people of this world, and all those who are involved directly or indirectly with the Education of different groups. Although efforts are required for a drastic change in the English Literature studies in India or in abroad, yet it will still take quite some time to get those proposals translated into reality.

In this context I would like to enunciate that the Capitalism or hoarding of resources at the center point it will not do the society's problems to be resolved in the near future. Resources are meant for all not for counted people in the segment of studies or with some Temple Estates, so called Gurus and so many types of property hoarders which are becoming gorgeously richer and richer and our poverty stricken people are in dearth of even two loaves of bread a day.

At one place, abundance of lavishness and aristocracy is prevailed and at another, there is nothing to be pulled on their life. This ingratitude must be worn out from the society of India. Now days, few people are busy with the hoarding of the cash and kind from all means. They don't have any thinking behind it that how the rest of the population will survive even with appropriate needs of the survival.

That is why the need to know the rudimentary rules and rubrics of law for all, as these is necessary. Much has been changing in general laws but nothing we find in shape of progress and prosperity. The basic tenet and underpinning philosophy of general laws is to protect the interests of the people by saving them from exploitation and harassment on one hand and providing enough leverage and stick of good governance to the Government so as to have conducive art of living culture on the other hand. The cordial and congenial relationship can be had only when both the limbs of society have better understanding in the light of the limits of their rights, responsibilities and duties.

As stated ibid, they are something serious rather than contextual but everything is fair in LOVE and WAR. Here love is for the public of India and war is against the cruel people of society who are behaving like blackcaps of India.

Most of the Indian professionals are unable to forget work while on a holiday, working up to three hours instead of enjoying the free time with family and friends. Developments in technology mean that students are always connected and the temptation to check emails and complete any tasks that follow on from them is easy to succumb to.

It does not matter that only a few in each generation will grasp and achieve the full reality of man's proper stature—and that the rest will betray it. It is those few that move the world and give life its meaning—and it is these few that we have always sought to address. The rest are no concern of mine; it is not me or all others that they will betray: it is their own souls.

Now, it is, I am hoping in very compassionate way that this book will be proved in positive manner, boon for the readers.

Faridabad
2013

Krishna Kumar Singh

SECTION TWO

ABBREVIATIONS

GLOSSARY OF MILITARY ABBREVIATIONS

List of terms, acronyms, information, related to modern armor, artillery, infantry, weapons, and related military subject matter.

A

AA - anti-aircraft

AAA - anti-aircraft artillery "Triple A"

AAAV - Advanced Amphibious Assault Vehicle

AAD - Armoured amphibious dozer

AAG - Anti-aircraft gun

AAK - Appliqué armour kit (US)

AAN - Army after next

AAPC - Advanced Armoured Personnel Carrier (Turkey)

AARADCOM - Army Armament Research and Development Command

AAR - After Action Review

AAV - Amphibious assault vehicle

AAV - Assault Amphibious Vehicle

AB - Air Burst

ABC - Atomic, biological, chemical

ABC - Automatic brightness control

AB(C) - Aviation battalion (combat)

ABIT - advanced built-in test

ABM - air bursting munitions

ABM - anti-ballistic missile

ABMS - air bursting ammunition system

ABRO - Army Base Repair Organisation

ABS - Aww-Busting System

ABS - anti-skid braking system

ABSV - Armoured Battle group Support Vehicle

A/C - aircraft commander

AC - alternating current

ACA - ammunition container assembly

ACAVP - Advanced Composite Armoured Vehicle Platform (UK)

ACCE - Abrams/Crusader Common Engine

ACCV – Armored Cavalry Cannon Vehicle (US)

ACE – Armored Combat Earthmover (US)

ACH – Advanced Combat Helmet

ACLOS-Automatic Command to Line of Sight

ACOG – Advanced Combat Optical Gun sight

ACP – Automatic Colt Pistol

ACR – Advanced Combat Rifle

ACR – Armored cavalry regiment

ACRV – Armoured command and reconnaissance vehicle

ACS – Artillery communications system

ACU – Army combat uniform

ACV – Aardvark Cleaning Vehicle (US)

ACV – Armoured combat vehicle

ACVT – Armored Combat Vehicle Technology Program (US)

ADA – air defense artillery

ADAM – Area Denial Artillery Munitions

ADAMS – Air Defense Advanced Mobile System (US)

ADATS – Air Defence Anti-Tank System

ADC-A – Assistant Division Commander – Fire and Maneuver

ADC-B – Assistant Division Commander – Combat Support

ADEA – Army Development and Employment Agency

ADI – Australian Defence Industries

AE – action express

AEF – Allied expeditionary force

AESA – Active electronically scanned array

AEV – Armoured engineer vehicle

AF – Air force

AFA/ARA – Aerial field artillery/aerial rocket artillery

AFARV – Armored, Forward Area, Re-arm Vehicle (US)

AFAS – advanced Field Artillery System

AFC – Australian Flying Corps

AFCS – automatic fire-control systems

AFD – automatic feeding device

AFSC – air force specialty code

AFSV – armoured fire support vehicle

AFV – Armored Family of Vehicles (US)

AFV – Armoured fighting vehicle

AGC – automatic gain control

AGF – Army ground forces

AGL – above ground level

AGL – automatic grenade launcher

AGLS – automatic gun laying system

AGS - armored gun system (US)

AGV - assault gun vehicle

AGVT - Advanced Ground Vehicle Technology

Ah - Ampere hour

AHC - Attack Helicopter Company (USA)

AICS - Accuracy International Chassis System

AICW - Advanced Individual Combat Weapon

AIF - Australian Imperial Force (Australia, WWI)

AIFS - Advanced Indirect Fire System

AIFV - Armoured infantry fighting vehicle

AIPS - Advanced Integrated Propulsion System (US)

ALAAVS - Advanced Light Armored/Amphibious Vehicle System (US)

ALC - Advanced Land Combat (US)

ALICE - All-purpose lightweight individual carrying equipment

ALS - Advanced laying system

ALSV - Armoured logistics support vehicle

ALT - Armoured launching turret

AMC - United States Army Material Command

AMC - Advanced Mortar Carrier (Turkey)

AMCCOM - Armament Munitions and Chemical Command

AMDS - Anti-Missile Discarding Sabot

AMF - Amphibische Mehrzweck- Fahrzeuge

AML - Automitrailleuse Légère (light armoured car)

AMLCD - Active-matrix liquid crystal display

AMOS - Advanced mortar system

AMR - Anti-materiel rifle

AMR - Automitrailleuse de Reconnaissance

AMRWS - Advanced multi-role weapon station

AMS - Armoured mortar system

AMS-H - Advanced Missile System - Heavy

AMX - Atelier de Construction daisy-les-Moulineaux

ANAD - Anniston Army Depot

ANZAC - Australia and New Zealand Army Corps

ANZUS - Australia New Zealand United States Treaty

AO - Area of operations

AOI - Arab Organisation for Industrialization

AOS - Add-on stabilization

AP - Anti-personnel

AP - Armour-piercing

APAM - Anti-personnel, antimateriel

APBC – Armour-piercing ballistic cap

APC – Armoured personnel carrier

APC – Armour-piercing capped

APCBC – Armour-piercing capped ballistic cap

APC-T – Armour-piercing capped – tracer

APCT-BF – Armour-piercing capped tracer – base fuse

APCNR – Armour-piercing composite non-rigid

APCR – Armour-piercing composite rigid

APCRBC – Armour-piercing composite rigid ballistic cap

APDS – Armour-piercing discarding sabot

APDS-T – Armour-piercing discarding sabot - tracer

APE – Amphibische Pionier-Erkundungsfahrzeug

APEP – Armour-Piercing Enhancement Programme

APERS – Anti-personnel

APERS-T – Anti-personnel tracer

APFIDS – Armour-piercing fragmentation incendiary discarding sabot

APFSDS-T – Armour-piercing fin-stabilized discarding sabot - tracer

APFSDS (P) - Armour-piercing fin-stabilized discarding sabot (practice)

APFSDSDU – Armour piercing fin-stabilized discarding sabot, depleted uranium

APG – Aberdeen Proving Grounds

APGM – Autonomous precision-guided munitions

APHC – Armour-piercing hard core

APHE – Armour-piercing high explosive

API – Armour-piercing incendiary

APIT – Armour-piercing incendiary tracer

APM – Anti-personnel mine

APS – Advanced propulsion system

APS – Artillery pointing system

APSA – Armour piercing secondary effect

APSE – Armour-piercing secondary effect

APSE-T – Armour-piercing secondary effect – tracer

APT – Armour-piercing tracer

APTE – Abrams Power Train Evolution (US)

APU – Auxiliary power unit

APV – Armoured patrol vehicle

AR – Assault rifle

AR/AAV – Armored Reconnaissance/Airborne Assault Vehicle (US)

ARD – Anti-reflective device

ARDEC – Armament Research,

Development and Engineering Center

ARDNOT - Automatic day/night optical tracker

ARE - Atelier de Construction Roanne

ARETS - Armour Remote Target System

ARFORGEN - Army force generation

ARMAD - Armoured and Mechanized Unit Air Defence

ARMSCOR - Armament Manufacturing Corporation (South Africa)

ARMVAL - Anti-armor vehicle evaluation (US)

ARP - Anti-radiation projectile

ARP - Armoured repair plates

ARRADCOM - Armament Research and Development Command

ARRV - Armoured repair and recovery vehicle

ARSV - Armored Reconnaissance Scout Vehicle (US)

ART - Armoured Recon Transport

ARV - Armoured recovery vehicle or Armed Robotic Vehicle

ASA-Advanced security agency

ASAP - As soon as possible

ASARC - Army Systems Acquisition Review Council

ASCOD - Austrian Spanish Cooperative Development

ASM - Armored Systems Modernization (US)

ASP - Automatic, self-powered

ASTROS - Artillery Saturation Rocket System (Brazil)

ASV - Armored Security Vehicle (US)

ASV - Ammunition supply vehicle

AT - Anti-tank

AT - Ape tape

ATACS - Advanced tank cannon system (US)

ATAS - Automatic target acquisition system

ATCAS - Advanced towed cannon system

ATD - Advanced technology demonstration

ATD - Advanced technology demonstrator (US)

ATD - Automatic target detection

ATDT - Automatic target detection and tracking

ATDU - Armoured Trials and Development Unit (UK)

ATFCS - Automated Targeting and Fire Control System

ATG - Anti-tank gun

ATGL - Anti-tank grenade launcher

ATGM - Anti-tank guided missile

ATGW - Anti-tank guided weapon

ATK - Alliant Techsystems

ATLAS - Advanced technology light artillery system

ATLV - Artillery target location vehicle

ATM - Anti-tank mine

ATR - - EDS Automotive test rig

ATS - Atelier de Construction de Tarbes

ATTC - All Terrain Tracked Carrier

ATTS - Air Transportable Towed System

ATV - All-terrain vehicle

ATV - Armoured TOW vehicle (Turkey)

AUG - Armee Universal Gewehr

AVGP - Armoured Vehicle General Purpose (Canada)

AVH - Armoured Vehicle Heavy

AVL - Armoured Vehicle Light

AVLB - Armoured vehicle-launched bridge

AVM - Armoured Vehicle Medium

AVR - Armoured vehicle reconnaissance

AVRE - Armoured Vehicle Royal Engineers (UK)

AVT - Advanced Vehicle Technologies (US)

AWE - Advanced Warfighting Experiment

AWOL - Absent without official leave

B

BAe - British Aerospace

BAR - Browning Automatic Rifle

BARV - Beach Armoured Recovery Vehicle

BASE - British Aerospace Systems and Equipment

BATES - Battlefield Artillery Target Engagement System

BAT - Biometrics Automated Toolset

BB - Base bleed

BBSP - Blowback shifted pulse

BC - Battery commander

BCC - battery control centre

BCP - Battery command post

BCT - Brigade combat team (US)

BCT - Basic combat training

BCV - Battle command vehicle

BD - base detonating

BDA - Browning double action or bomb damage assessment

BDM - Bunker demolition munitions

BDU - Battle dress uniform

BE - Base ejection

BFA - Blank-firing adaptor or blank-firing attachment

BFV - Bradley Fighting Vehicle

BGT - Brigade combat team

BHP - Brake horsepower

BIFF - Battlefield identification friend or foe

BILL - Bofors, infantry, light and lethal

BITE - Built-in test equipment

BL - Blank

BL-T - Black tracer

BLITS - Beta lighted infantry telescope system

BLT - Battalion landing team

BLR - Blind ado Ligero de Ruedas

BMF - Belgian Mechanical Fabrication

BMNT - Begin morning nautical twilight

BMP - Pronounced "bimp"

BMR - Blind ado Medio de Ruedas

BMS - Battalion mortar system

BMS - Battlefield management system

BNCC (USAF) - Base network control center

BNS - Bill night sight

BOCV - Battery operations centre vehicle

BOG-Dwell - Boots on the ground - dwells

BOL - Bearing-only launch

BOLTS - Bolt-on loading tray system

BOSS - Ballistic optimizing shooting system

BPS - Battery power source

BSP - Bright source protection

BSSG - Brigade service support group

BST - Basic skills trainer

BT - Boat tail

BT - Bullet trap

BTA - Best technical approach

BTU - Bullet trap universal

BUA - BILL under armour or built-up area

BW - Bacteriological warfare

BX - Bionix AFV

C

C3I - Command, control, communications, and intelligence

CAB - Combat aviation battalion

CAD - Computer-assisted design

CAG - Commander of the Air Group

CAL - Canadian Arsenals Limited

CAP - Civil air patrol

CAP - Combat air patrol

CAP - Combustible augmented plasma

CARRV - Challenger armoured repair and recovery vehicle

CAS - Close air support

CASEVAC - Casualty evacuation

CAT/FCS - Command adjusted trajectory/fire-control system (US)

CAT/LCV - Combined arms team/lightweight combat vehicle (US)

CATT - Combined arms tactical trainer (UK)

CATT-B - Component Advanced Technology TestBed (US)

CAV - Composite armored vehicle (US)

CAWS - Cannon Artillery Weapons Systems (US)

CAX - Combined arms exercise

CBR - Chemical, biological, radiological

CBRN - Chemical, biological, radiological, nuclear

CCC - Combustible cartridge case

CCD - Charge-coupled device

CCO - Close combat optic

CCP - Computer control panel

CCR - Crown copyright reserved

CCTV - Closed-circuit television

CCU - Central control unit

CCV - Close combat vehicle

CCV - Command and control vehicle (US)

CCV-L - Close combat vehicle - light

CD - candela

CDA - Combat defensive action

CDM - Coastal defence missile

CDU - Command display unit

CDU - Computer display unit

CE - Chemical energy

C/E - Crew/enlisted

CECOM - Communications-electronics command

CEFO - Combat equipment fighting order

CENTCOM - Central command

CENTO - Central Treaty Organisation or Baghdad Pact

CEOI - Communications electronics operating instruction

CEP - Circular error of probability

CEPP - Controlled effect police projectile

CET - Combat engineer tractor

CEU - Computer electronics unit

CEV - Combat engineer vehicle

CF - Canadian Forces

CF - Controlled fragmentation

CFE - Conventional forces Europe

CFV - Cavalry fighting vehicle (US)

CG - Commanding general

CGS - Crew gunnery simulator

CHA - Cast homogeneous armour

CHARM - Challenger chieftain armament

CHIP - Challenger improvement programme

CIFV - Composite infantry fighting vehicle

CILAS - Compagnie Industrielle des Lasers

CIS - Chartered Industries of Singapore

CIS - Commonwealth of Independent States

CITV - Commander's independent thermal viewer (US)

CIWS - Close-in weapons system

CLAMS - Clear lane marking system (US)

CLASS - Computerized Laser Sight System

CLAWS - Close combat light armor weapon system (US)

CLGP - Cannon-launched guided projectile (US)

CLOS - Command to line of sight

CLU - Command launch unit

CM - Colour-marking or "continue mission"

CMS - Common missile system

CMS - Compact modular sight

CMT - Cadmium-mercury telluride

CMV - Combat mobility vehicle (US)

CNVD - Clip-on night vision device

COB - Close of business

CO - Commanding officer

COG - Course over ground

Comp - B Composition B

COMVAT - Combat vehicles armament technology (US)

COMZ - Communications zone

COP - Combat out post

COS - Chief of section

COSCOM - Corps support command (US Army)

COFS - Chief of staff

COTAC - Conduite de Tir Automatique pour Char

COTS - Commercial-off-the-shelf

COV - Counter obstacle vehicle (US)

CP - Concrete-piercing

CPR - Common practice round

CPS - Cardinal points specification (UK)

CPV - Command post vehicle

CQB - Close quarters battle

CQBW - Close-quarters battle weapon

CR - Capability requirement

CRISAT - Collaborative research into small arms technology

CRM - Composite risk management (US)

CROWS - Common Remotely Operated Weapon Station

CRR - Carro de Reconhecimento Sobre Rodas

CRT - Cathode ray tube

CRU - Cable reel unit

CS - Communications subsystem

CS - Confined space

CS (USAF) - Communications squadron

CSB - Combat support boat

CSF - Combined service forces

CSI - computer-synthesized image

CSS - Computer sighting system

CSSD - Combat service support detachment

CTA - Case telescoped ammunition

CTD - Concept technology demonstrator

CTI - Central tyre inflation

CTIS - Central tyre inflation system

CTO - Central Treaty Organisation or Baghdad Pact

CTR - Close Target Recce

CTRA - Carro de Transporte Sobre Rodas Anfibo

CTT - Challenger training tank

CV90 - Combat Vehicle 90

CVAST - Combat vehicle armament system technology (US)

CVR(T) - Combat vehicle reconnaissance (tracked) (UK)

CVR(W) - Combat vehicle reconnaissance (wheeled) (UK)

CVRDE - Combat vehicle research and development establishment (India)

CVT - Controlled variable time

CVTTS - Combat vehicle targeting system

CW - Chemical warfare

CWR - Continuous wave radar

CWS - Cupola weapon station

D

DA - double action

DAHA - dual-axis head assembly

DAO - double action only

DARCOM - US Army Matériel Development and Readiness Command

DAREOD - damaged airfield reconnaissance explosive ordnance disposal

DARPA - Defense Advanced Research Projects Agency (US)

DAS - deep air support

DAS - defensive aid system/suite

DASP - demountable artillery surveillance pod

DBMS - dead bodies make sense

DC - direct current

DCA - défense contre avions

DCCT - dismounted close combat trainer

DD - Detroit diesel

DDA - Detroit Diesel Allison

DDS - Department of Defense Support

DDU - digital display unit

DECA - digital electronic control assembly

DEFA - direction des études et fabrications d'armement

DERA - Defence Evaluation and Research Agency (UK)

DESO - Defence Export Sales Organisation (UK)

DFAC - Dining Facility (US)

DFCS - digital fire-control system

DFSV - direct fire support vehicle

DFV - desert fighting vehicle

DHSS - data handling subsystem

DIA - Defense Intelligence Agency (US)

DICON - Defence Industries Corporation of Nigeria

DIP - driver instrument panel

DISA - Defense Information Systems Agency

DISCOM - division support command

DIVARTY - division artillery

DMC - digital magnetic compass

DMR - dedicated marksman rifle

DMU - distance measurement unit

DNRS - day/night range sight

DoD - Department of Defense (US)

DOIM (US Army) - Directorate of Information Management

DOP - Department of Productivity

DP - demonstration purpose

DP - dual purpose

DPA - Defence Procurement Agency (UK)

DPICM - dual-purpose improved conventional munitions (US)

DPTR - diopter

DRA - Defence Research Agency (UK)

DROPS - demountable rack offloading and pick-up system

DS/T - practice discarding sabot/tracer

DSACS - direct support armored cannon system (US)

DSETS - direct support electrical test system

DSO - Defence Sales Organisation

DSRV - Deep Submergence Rescue Vehicle (US)

DSWS - Division Support Weapon System

DTAT - Direction Technique des Armements Terrestres

DTT - driver training tank

DU - depleted uranium

DV - demining vehicle

DVE - driver's vision enhancer

DWFK - deep water fording kit

E

EAAK - Enhanced Appliqué Armor Kit (US)

EAOS - Enhanced Artillery Observation System

EBG - Engin Blindé Génie (armoured combat vehicle)

EBR - Engin Blindé de Reconnaissance

EBRC - Engine Blindé à roues de Contact

EC - Enhanced Carbine

ECM - Electronic countermeasures

ECOS - Enhanced Combat Optical Sight

ECS - Environmental Control Subsystem

ECV - Enhanced Capacity Vehicle

EDD - Explosive Detonation Disruption

EDS - Electric Drive System

EFAB - Establishment d'Etudes et de Fabrications d'Armement de Bourges

EFC - equivalent full charge

EFCR - equivalent full charge rounds

EFM - Explosives Factory Maribyrnong

EFP - Expanded Feasibility Phase

EFP - Explosively Formed Penetrator

EFV - Expeditionary Fighting Vehicle

EFVS - Electronic Fighting Vehicle System (US)

EG - External Gun

EGLM - Enhanced Grenade Launcher Module

EI - Engineering and Installation

EIS - Engineering and Installation Squadron

EI SIT - Engineering and Installation Site Implementation Team

ELB - Extended Life Barrel

ELKE - Elevated Kinetic Energy Weapon (US)

ELS - Electromagnetic Launcher System

ELSAP - Elektronische Schiessanlage für Panzer

EM - electromagnetic

EMC - Executive Management Committee

EMD - Engineering and Manufacturing Development

EMDG - Euromissile Dynamics Group

EMEW - Electromagnetically-Augmented High Explosive Warhead

EMG - externally mounted gun

EMP - electromagnetic pulse

EMPG - Electromagnetic Pulse Grenade

ENGESA - Engesa Engenheiros Especializados (Brazil)

EOC - Essential Operational Capability

EOD - explosive ordnance disposal

EOR - Explosive Ordnance Reconnaissance

EOTS - Electro-Optical Tracking System

EPC - electronic plane conversion

EPC - Engin Principal de Combat

EPG - Enhanced Performance Grenade

EPG - European Production Group

EPG - European Programme Group

EPS - Electrical Power Subsystem

EPU - Electronics Processing Unit

ER - enhanced radiation

ER - extended range

ERA - explosive reactive armour

ERA - extended range ammunition

ERC - Engin de Reconnaissance Canon

ERFB - extended range full-bore

ERFB-BB - extended range full-bore - base bleed

ERGFCDS - Extended Range Gunnery Fire-Control Demonstration System

ERGP - extended range guided projectile

ERMIS - Extended Range Modification Integration System

ERP - Extended Range Projectile

ERSC - extended range subcalibre

ERV - emergency rescue vehicle

ERV - Engineer Reconnaissance Vehicle

ES - Extreme Spread

ESAF - Electronic Safety and Arm Function

ESD - Electronique Serge Dassault

ESLDE - Eyesafe Laser Daylight Elbow

ESPAWS - Enhanced Self-Propelled Artillery Weapon System (US)

ESRS - electro-slag refined steel

ETA - Estimated Time of Arrival

ETC - Electro Thermal Cannon

ETD - Estimated Time of Departure

ETM - Electronic Technical Manuals

ETS - Elevated TOW System

ETS - Engineer Tank System

EW - electronic warfare

EWK - Eisenwerke Kaiserslautern Göppner

EWS - external weapon station

F

FAAD – Forward Area Air Defense

FAAR – Forward Area Alerting Radar (US)

FAARP – Forward Area Arming & Refueling Point

FAASV – Field Artillery Ammunition Support Vehicle (US)

FAC – Forward Air Control(er)

FAC-A – Forward Air Control(er)-Airborne

FACE – Field Artillery Computer Equipment

FAL – Fusil Automatique Légère

FAPDS – Frangible Armour-Piercing Discarding Sabot

FARP – Forward Area Refueling Point

FARS – field artillery rocket system

FARV-A – Future Armored Resupply Vehicle - Artillery (US)

FAST – Forward Area Support Team

FAV – Fast Attack Vehicle (US)

FBI – Federal Bureau of Investigation

FBRV – Future Beach Recovery Vehicle (UK)

FCC – Fire Command Centre

FCC – Fire-Control Computer

FCCVS – Future Close-Combat Vehicle System (US)

FCE – fire-control equipment

FCLV – Future Command and Liaison Vehicle (UK)

FCS – fire-control system/subsystem

FCS – Future Combat System

FCU – Fire Control Unit

FDC – fire direction centre

FDCV – fire direction centre vehicle

FDSWS – Future Direct Support Weapon System

FEBA – Forward Edge of the Battle Area

FEP – Firepower Enhancement Programme

FET – Future Engineer Tank

FFAR – Folding Fin Aerial Rocket

FFE – Fire for Effect

FFSS – Future Fighting Soldier System

FG – field gun

FH – field howitzer

FIBUA – Fighting In Built-Up Areas

FID – Foreign Internal Defenses

FIFV – Future Infantry Fighting Vehicle (US)

FIRM – Floating Integrated Rail Mount

FIS – Fuse Interface System

FISH – Fighting In Someone's House (UK)

FIST – Future Integrated Soldier Technology (UK)

FISTV – Fire Support Team Vehicle (US)

FITOW – Further Improved TOW (US)

FLEA – Frangible Low-Energy Ammunition

FLIR – forward-looking infrared

FLOT – forward line of own troops

FLSW – Future Light Support Weapon

FM – U.S. Army Field Manuals

FM – Titanium tetrachloride

FMBS – Family of Muzzle Brake/Suppressors

FMC – Food Machinery Corporation

FMF – Fleet Marine Force

FMJ – Full Metal Jacket

FMJBT – Full Metal Jacket Boat Tail

FMJLF – Full Metal Jacket Lead Free

FMS – Foreign Military Sales

FMTV – Family of Medium Tactical Vehicles

FN – Fabrique Nationale

FO – Forward Observer

FOB – Forward Operating Base

FOC – Full Operational Capability

FOD – Foreign Object Damage

FOG – Fibre Optic Gyro

FOM – Fibre Optic Missile

FOO – forward observation officer

FORTIS – Forward Observation and Reconnaissance Thermal Imaging System

FOTT – Follow On To TOW

FOV – field of view

FPA – Focal Plane Array

FRAG – fragmentation

FRAGO – Fragmentary Order

FRES – Future Rapid Effect System

FROG – free rocket over ground

FSCL – fire support coordination line

FSCM – fire support coordination measure

FSCV – fire support combat vehicle

FSE – fire support element

FSED – full-scale engineering development (US)

FSSG – Force Service Support Group

FST – Future Soviet Tank/Follow-on Soviet Tank

FSV – fire support vehicle

FSV – Future Scout Vehicle (US)

FTA – Frangible Training Ammunition

FTMA – Future Tank Main Armament

FTS – Future Tank Study

FTT – Field Tactical Trainer

FUBAR – Fouled/Fucked Up Beyond All Reason/Recognition/Repair

FUE – First Unit Equipped

FUG – Felderitö Usó Gépkosci

FV – fighting vehicle

FV/GCE – fighting vehicle gun control equipment

FVDD – Fighting Vehicle Development Division

FVRDE – Fighting Vehicle Research and Development Establishment (UK)

FVS – Fighting Vehicle System (US)

FVSC – Fighting Vehicle Systems Carrier (US)

FY – fiscal year

G

g – Gramme (s)

G – Gendarmerie

GAMA – Gun Automatic Multiple Ammunition

GAO – General Accounting Office

GAP – Gun Aiming Post

GBAD – Ground Based Air Defence

GCE – gun control equipment

GCT – Grande Cadence de Tir (high rate of fire)

GCU – Gun Control Unit

GCW – Gross Combat Weight

GD – General Dynamics

GDLS – General Dynamics Land Systems

GDU – Gun Display Unit

GFE – Government Furnished Equipment

GH – gun-howitzer

GIAT – Groupement Industriel des Armements Terrestres

GL – Grenade Launcher

GLATGM – Gun Launched Anti-Tank Guided Missile

GLC – gun lay computer

GLDNSM – Grenade Launcher Day-Night Sight Mount

GLH-H – Ground-Launched Hellfire-Heavy (US)

GLLD – Ground Laser Locator Designator (US)

GLS – Gesellschaft für Logistischen Service

GM, MVO – General Motors, Military Vehicle Operations

GMC – General Motors Corporation

GMG – Grenade Machine Gun

GMLRS – Guided Multiple Launch Rocket System

GMS – Gun Management System

GOCO – government-owned, contractor-operated (US)

GOP – General Out Post

GP – General Purpose

GP – guided projectile

GPMG – General Purpose Machine Gun

GPO - gun position officer

GPS - Global Positioning System

GPS - gunner's primary sight

GPSS - Gunner's Primary Sight Subsystem

GREM - Grenade Rifle Entry Munitions

GRU - Glavnoe Razvedyvatel'noe Upravlenie

GSR - General Staff Requirement (US)

GSRS - General Support Rocket System

GST - General Staff Target

GST - Gesellschaft für System-Technik

GTCS - Gun Test and Control System

GTI - German Tank Improvement

GVW - Gross Vehicle Weight

GW - guided weapon

H

h - Hour (s)

H&K - Heckler and Koch

HAB - Heavy Assault Bridge (US)

HAG - Heavy Artillery Gun

HALO - High Altitude Low Opening

HAMS - Headquarters and Maintenance Squadron

HAWK - Homing-All-the-Way-Killer (US)

HB - heavy barrel

HBAR - Heavy Barrel Assault Rifle

HC - Hexachloroethane/zinc

HC - high-capacity

HC - Hollow Charge

HCER - high-capacity extended range

HCHE - high-capacity high-explosive

HCT - HOT Compact Turret

HDS - Holographic Diffraction Sight

HE - high-explosive

HE-APERS - high-explosive anti-personnel

HE-FRAG - high-explosive fragmentation

HE-FRAG-FS - high-explosive fragmentation - fin-stabilized

HE-FS - high-explosive - fin-stabilized

HE-S - high-explosive spotting

HE-T - high-explosive tracer

HE/PR - high-explosive practice

HEAA - High-Explosive Anti-Armour

HEAB - High-Explosive Air Burst

HEAP - High-Explosive Armor-Piercing

HEAP-T - high-explosive anti-personnel - tracer

HEAT - high-explosive anti-tank

HEAT-FS – high-explosive anti-tank fin-stabilized

HEAT-MP – high-explosive anti-tank multipurpose

HEAT-MP (P) – high-explosive anti-tank multipurpose (practice)

HEAT-T – high-explosive anti-tank - tracer

HEAT-T-HVY – high-explosive anti-tank - tracer - heavy

HEAT-T-MP – high-explosive anti-tank - tracer - multipurpose

HEAT-TP-T – high-explosive anti-tank - target practice - tracer

HED-D – Hybrid Electric Drive - Demonstrator

HEDP – high-explosive dual-purpose

HEER – High-Explosive Extended Range (US)

HEF – High-Explosive Fragmentation

HEFT – High-Explosive Follow Through

HEI – high-explosive incendiary

HEIT – high-explosive incendiary tracer

HEL – High-Energy Laser (US)

HEL – Human Engineering Laboratory (US)

HELP – Howitzer Extended Life Program (US)

HEMAT – Heavy Expanded Mobility Ammunition Trailer (US)

HEMP – High-Explosive Multi-Purpose

HEMTT – Heavy Expanded Mobility Tactical Truck (US)

HEP – high-explosive plastic

HEP-T – high-explosive practice - tracer

HEPD – high-explosive point detonating

HERA – high-explosive rocket-assisted

HESH – high-explosive squash head

HESH-T – high-explosive squash head - tracer

HET-PF – high-explosive tracer - percussion fuse

HETF – High Explosive Time Fuzed

HETS – Heavy Equipment Transport System

HFCC – Howitzer Fire-Control Computer (US)

HFHTB – Human Factors Howitzer TestBed (US)

HFM – Heavy Force Modernization (US)

HIFV – Heavy Infantry Fighting Vehicle

HIMAG – High-Mobility Agility Test Vehicle (US)

HIMARS – High-Mobility Artillery Rocket System (US)

HIP – Howitzer Improvement Program (US)

HIRE – Hughes Infrared Equipment

HITP – High-Ignition Temperature Propellant

HIU – Heading Indicator Unit

HMC – Howitzer Motor Carriage

HMD – Helmet-Mounted Display

HMG – Heavy Machine Gun

HMH – Marine Heavy Helicopter Squadron

HMLC – High-Mobility Load Carrier

HML/A – Marine Light/Attack Helicopter Squadron

HMM – Marine Medium Helicopter Squadron

HMMWV – High Mobility Multipurpose Wheeled Vehicle

HMX – Marine Special Mission Helicopter Squadron

HOE – Holographic Optical Element

HOT – Haute subsonique Optiquement Téléguidé

How – Howitzer

HP – High Power; Hollow Point

Hp – Horsepower

HPFP – High-Performance Fragmentation Projectile

HPS – Helmet Pointing System (or Sight)

HPT – high-pressure test

HRU – Heading Reference Unit

HS – Headquarters Squadron - Marine Wing Support Group (USMC)

HSS – Hunter Sensor Suite

HSTV (L) – High-Survivability Test Vehicle (Lightweight) (US)

HTTB – High-Technology TestBed (US)

HVAP – high-velocity armour-piercing

HVAP-T – high-velocity armour-piercing tracer

HVAPDS-T – high-velocity armour-piercing discarding sabot - tracer

HVAPFSDS – high-velocity armour-piercing fin-stabilized discarding sabot

HVCC – High Velocity Canister Cartridge

HVM – Hypervelocity Missile

HVSS – horizontal volute spring suspension

HVSW – Hypervelocity Support Weapon

HVTP-T – high-velocity target practice - tracer

HWSTD – High Water Speed Technology Demonstrator

HYPAK – Hydraulic Power Assist Kit

I

I – Incendiary

IAFV – infantry armoured fighting vehicle

IAI – Israel Aircraft Industries

IAL – Infra-red Aiming Light

IASD – Instant Ammunition Selection Device

IBAS – Improved Bradley Acquisition System

ICC – information co-ordination centre

ICM – improved conventional munitions

ICM – BB improved conventional monition base bleed

ICV – Infantry Combat Vehicle

IDF – Israel Defense Forces

IDW – Individual Defence Weapon

IED – Improvised Explosive Device

IEPG – Independent European Program Group

IFCS – Improved/Integrated Fire-Control System

IFF – Identification Friend or Foe

IFV – infantry fighting vehicle

IFVwCM – Infantry Fighting Vehicle with Integrated Countermeasures (US)

IGLS – Individual Grenade Launcher System

II – image intensification/intensifier

IIR – Imaging Infra-Red

ILL – illuminating

ILMS – Improved Launcher Mechanical System

ILS – Integrated Logistic Support

IM – Insensitive Monition(s)

IMMLC – Improved Medium Mobility Load Carrier

IMU – Inertial Measurement Unit

INSAS – Indian Small Arms System

InSb – Indium-antimonide

IOC – initial operational capability

IOF – Indian Ordnance Factory

IPB – Intelligence Preparation of the Battlefield

IPF – Initial Production Facility

IPO – International Programme Office

IPPD – Integrated Product Process Development

IR – Infra-Red

IRBM – Intermediate-range ballistic missile

IRU – Inertial Reference Unit

IS – internal security

ISD – In Service Date

ISGU – Integrated Sight and Guidance Unit

ISR – Intelligence Surveillance and Reconnaissance

ISU – Integrated Sight Unit

ISV – Internal Security Vehicle

ITAS – Improved Target Acquisition System

ITOW – Improved TOW

ITPIAL – Infra-red Target Pointer/Illuminator/Aiming Laser

ITT – Invitation To Tender

ITV – Improved TOW Vehicle (US)

IVPDL - Inter-Vehicle Positioning and Data Link (US)

IW - Individual Weapon

IWS - Improved Weapon System

J

JBMoU - Joint Ballistic Memorandum of Understanding

JDAM - Joint Direct Attack Monition

JERRV - Joint Engineer Rapid Response Vehicle

JGSDF - Japanese Ground Self-Defence Force

JHP - Jacketed hollow point

JLTA - Javelin Composite Launch Tube

JMAC - Joint Medium-caliber Automatic Cannon

JPO - Joint Project Office

JSC - Joint Steering Committee

JSCS - Joint Service Combat Shotgun

JSDFA - Japanese Self-Defence Force Agency

JSP - Jacketed Soft Point

JSSAMP - Joint Services Small Arms Master Plan

JSSAP - Joint Services Small Arms Programme

K

KAAV - Korean Armoured Amphibious Vehicle

KAC - Knight's Armament Company

KE - Kinetic energy

KEC - Kaman Electromagnetics Corporation

KEM - Kinetic Energy Missile (US)

kg - kilogramme(s)

KIA - Killed in Action

KIFV - Korean Infantry Fighting Vehicle

KPA - Korean People's Army

L

LAAG - light anti-aircraft gun

LAAM - Light Anti-Aircraft Missile

LAAW - Light Anti-Tank Assault Weapon

LACA - Landing Craft Air Cushion

LAD - light aid detachment

LADS - light air defense system (US)

LAG - Light Artillery Gun

LALO - Low Altitude Low Opening

LAM - Laser Aiming Module

LAPES - Low-Altitude Parachute Extraction System

LAR - Light Automatic Rifle

LASER - Light Amplification by Stimulated Emission of Radiation

LASIP - Light Artillery System Improvement Plan

LATS – Light Armoured Turret System

LAU – Light Armoured Unit

LAV – Light Armored Vehicle (US)

LAV – Light Assault Vehicle (US)

LAV-AD – Light Armored Vehicle - Air Defense

LAW – light anti-tank weapon

LB – Long Barrel

LC – Laser Collimator

LCD – Liquid crystal display

LCS – Loader Control System

LCU – Landing Craft Utility

LCV – Light Contingency Vehicle (LCV) (US)

LD – Low drag, Line of Departure

LE – Law Enforcement

LED – light emitting diode

LEP – Life Extension Programme

LEU – Launcher Erector Unit

LF – ATGW Light Forces' Anti-Tank Guided Weapon

LF – Linked Feed

LFHG – Lightweight Fragmentation Hand Grenade

LFL – Light Fighter Lethality

LIA – Linear Induction Accelerator

LIMAWS – Lightweight Mobile Artillery Weapon System

LION – Lightweight Infra-red Observation Night sight

LIW – Lyttleton Engineering Works

LKP – Loader Keyboard Panel

LLAD – low-level air defence

LLLTV – low light level television

LLM – Launcher Loader Module

LMAW – Light Multi-purpose Assault Weapon

LMG – light machine gun

LNS – Land Navigation System

LNS – Laying and Navigation System

L/O – Liaison Officer

LOAL – Lock-On after Launch

LOBL – Lock-On before Launch

LOC – Line Of Communication

LOS – Line Of Sight

LOSAT – Line Of Sight Anti-Tank

LP – Liquid Propellant

LP – Listening Post

LPC – Launch Pod Container

LPC – Launcher Pod Carrier

LPG – Liquid Propellant Gun

LPO – Leading Petty Officer

LPT – Low-Profile Turret

LPTS – Lightweight Protected Turret System

LR – Long Rifle

LR – Long-Range

LRAR – Long Range Artillery Rocket

LRASS – Long-Range Advanced Scout System

LRAT - long-range anti-tank

LRBB - long-range base bleed

LRD - Long Range Deflagrator

LRF - laser rangefinder

LRF - Low Recoil Force

LRHB - long-range hollow base

LRIP - Low-Rate Initial Production

LRM - Laser Rangefinder Module

LRN - Lead Round Nose

LRN - Low Recoil NORICUM

LRRP - Long Range Reconnaissance Patrol

LRSA - Long Range Sniper Ammunition

LRSU - Long Range Surveillance Unit

LRU - Launcher Replenishment Unit

LRU - Line Replacement Unit

LRU - Line-Replaceable Unit

LSB - Landing Support Battalion

LSS - Lightweight Shotgun System

LSW - Light Support Weapon

LTA - Launch Tube Assembly

LTD - Laser Target Designator

LTFCS - Laser Tank Fire-Control System

LTP - Laser Target Pointer, Luminesant Training Projectile

LUTE - Lightweight Uncooled Thermal Imager Equipment

LVA - landing vehicle assault (US)

LVS - Lightweight Video Sight

LVT - Landing Vehicle Tracked (US)

LVTC - Landing Vehicle Tracked Command (US)

LVTE - Landing Vehicle Tracked Engineer (US)

LVTH - Landing Vehicle Tracked Howitzer (US)

LVTP - Landing Vehicle Tracked Personnel (US)

LVTR - Landing Vehicle Tracked Recovery (US)

LWC - Lead Wad Cutter

LWIR - Long Wave Infrared

LWL - Lightweight Launcher

LWML - Lightweight Multiple Launcher

LWMS - Lightweight Modular Sight

LWS - laser warning system

LWT - light weapon turret

LZ - landing zone

M

m - Meter (s)

M/s - metres per second

MAB - Marine Amphibious Brigade

MABS - Marine Air Base Squadron

MAC - Medium Armored Car (US)

MAC - Military Airlift Command

MACS - Modular Artillery Charge System

MACS - Marine Air Control Squadron

MADLS - Mobile Air Defence Launching System

MAF - Marine Amphibious Force

MAG - Marine Aircraft Group

MAGTEC - Marine Air/Ground Training & Education Command

MAGTF - Marine Air/Ground Task Force

MAHEM - Magnetohydrodynamic Explosive Munitions

MALOS - Miniature Laser Optical Sight

MALS - Marine Air Logistics Squadron

MAMBA - Mobile Artillery Monitoring Battlefield Radar

MANPADS - Man Portable Air Defense System

MAOV - Mobile Artillery Observation Vehicle

MAP - Military Aid Programme

MAPS - Modular Azimuth Position System

MAR - Micro Assault Rifle

MARDI - Mobile Advanced Robotics Defence Initiative (UK)

MARDIV - Marine Division (US)

MARS - Military Amateur Radio Station

MARS - Mini Assault Rifle System

MARS - Multi-purpose Aiming Reflex Sight

MARS - Multiple Artillery Rocket System

MASS - Marine Air Support Squadron

MATCS - Marine Air Traffic Control Squadron

MATSG - Marine Air Training Support Group

MAU (SOC) - Marine Amphibious Unit (Special Operations Capable)

MAV - maintenance assist vehicle

MAVD - MLRS Aim Verification Device

MAW - Marine Air Wing (US)

MBA - main battle area

MBB - Messerschmitt-Bölkow-Blohm

MBC - Mortar Ballistic Computer

MBT - main battle tank

MCLOS - Manual Command to Line Of Sight

MCRV - Mechanized Combat Repair Vehicle

MCS - Microclimate Conditioning System

MCS - modular charge system

MCSK - Mine Clearance System Kit (US)

MCT - Medium Combat Tractor (US)

MCT - Mercury Cadmium Telluride

MCV - Mechanized Combat Vehicle

MCWL - Marine Corps Warfighting Laboratory

MCWS - Minor Calibre Weapons Station (US)

MDMP - Military Decision Making Process

MDU - Map Display Unit

MEB - Marine Expeditionary Brigade

MEDEVAC - Medical Evacuation

MEF - Marine Expeditionary Force

MENS - Mission Element Need Statement (US)

MEP - Modular Explosive Penetrator

MEPS-Military Entrance Processing Station

METO - Middle East Treaty Organisation

METL - Mission Essential Task List

METT-TC - Mission, Enemy, Terrain and weather, Troops and support available – Time available, Civilians

MEU (SOC) - Marine Expeditionary Unit (Special Operations Capable)

MEV - medical evacuation vehicle (US)

MEWS - Mobile Electronic Warfare System

MEWSS - Mobile Electronic Warfare Support System

MF - multifunction

MFC - Mortar Fire Control (ler)

MFCS - Multi-Fire Control System

MFCV - Missile Fire-Control Vehicle

MFF - munitions filling factory

MG - machine gun

MGB - Medium Girder Bridge

MGL - Multiple Grenade Launchers

MGS - Mobile Gun System

MGTS - MultiGun Turret System

MGU - Mid-course Guidance Unit

MI - Military Intelligence

MIA - Missing In Action

MICOM - Missile Command (US)

MICV - mechanized infantry combat vehicle

MILAN - Missile d'Infantrie Léger Antichar

MILES - Multiple Integrated Laser Engagement System (US)

MILSPEC - Military Specification

MILSTAR - Military Strategic and Tactical Relay (US)

MIPS – Medium Integrated Propulsion System (US)

MLA – Manufacturing Licence Agreement

MLC – Military Load Class

MLC – Modular Load Carrier

MLF – Marine Logistics Force

MLR – Marine Logistics Regiment

MLI – Mid-Life Improvement

MLO – Muzzle Loaded Ordnance

MLRS – Multiple Launch Rocket System (US)

mm – millimeter(s)

MMBF – mean miles between failures

MMG – Medium Machine Gun

MMS – mast-mounted sight

MMS – Modular Mounting System

MNVD – Monocular Night Vision Device

MoA – Memorandum of Agreement

MOA – Minute Of Angle

MoD – Ministry of Defence

MODA – Ministry of Defence and Aviation

MOLF – Modular Laser Fire Control (Germany)

MOLLE – MOdular Lightweight Load-carrying Equipment

MOPP – Mission Oriented Protective Posture (US)

MOS – Military Occupational Specialty (US)

MoU – Memorandum of Understanding

MOUT – Military Operations in Urban Terrain (US)

MP – Machine Pistol

MPBAV – Multipurpose Base Armoured Vehicle

MPC – Multipurpose Carrier (Netherlands)

MPGS – Mobile Protected Gun System (US)

MPI – Mean Point of Impact

MPIM – Multipurpose Individual Munitions

MPM – Multipurpose Munitions

MPS – Maritime Prepositioning Ships (US)

MPV – Multi-Purpose Vehicle

MPWS – Mobile Protected Weapon System (US)

MR – Medium Range

MRAP – Mine Resistant Ambush Protected (Vehicle)

MRAR – MultiRole Assault Round

MRAV – MultiRole Armoured Vehicle

MRBF – mean rounds before failure

MRBS – mean rounds between stoppages

MRE – Meal Ready to Eat

MRS – multiple rocket system

MRS - muzzle reference system

MRSI - Multiple Round Simultaneous Impact

MRV(R) - Mechanized Recovery Vehicle (Repair)

MRVR - Mechanized Repair and Recovery Vehicle (US)

MSSG - MAU/MEU Service Support Group (USMC)

MSR - Missile Simulation Round

MSR - Main Supply Route

MSTAR - Man-portable Surveillance and Target Acquisition Radar

MSV - Modular Support Vehicle

MT - mechanical time

MTB - Mobility TestBed

MTBF - Mean Time between Failures

MTI - moving target indication

MTL - Materials Technology Laboratory (US)

MTR - Mobile Test Rig (US)

MTSQ - mechanical time and super-quick

MTSQ - Mechanical Time Semi-Quick

MTU - Motoren- und Turbinen-Union

MTVL - mobile tactical vehicle light

MUGS - Multipurpose Universal Gunner Sight

MULE - Modular Universal Laser Equipment (US)

MUSS - Multifunctional Self-protection System

MV - muzzle velocity

MVEE - Military Vehicles and Engineering Establishment (UK)

MVRS - Muzzle Velocity Radar System

MWCS - Marine Wing Communications Squadron

MWHS - Marine Wing Headquarters Squadron

MWS - Manned Weapon Station (US)

MWS - Modular Weapon System

MWSG - Marine Wing Support Group

MWSS - Marine Wing Support Squadron

N

NATO - North Atlantic Treaty Organisation

NBC - Nuclear, Biological, Chemical

NBMR - NATO Basic Military Requirement

NCIS - Naval Criminal Investigative Service (US)

NCO - Non-Commissioned Officer (US, E-4 - E-9)

NCOIC - Non-Commissioned Officer in Charge

NDI - Non-Developmental Item

NDU - Navigation Display Unit

NFOV - Narrow Field of View

NG – New/Next Generation

Ni/Cd – Nickel Cadmium

NLAW – Next Light (weight) Anti-armour Weapon

NLOS-C – Non-Line of Sight-Cannon

NLOS-M – Non-Line of Sight-Mortar

NOD(s) - Night Optical Device(s)

NRF – NATO Response Force

NS – Network Services

NTC – National Training Center (USA)

NUGP – nominal unit ground pressure

NV – Night Vision

NVD – Night Vision Device

NVE – Night Vision Equipment

NVESD – Night Vision and Electronic Sensors Directorate

NVG – Night Vision Goggle

NVS – Night Vision System

NZDF – New Zealand Defence Force

NZEF – New Zealand Expeditionary Force

O

OBR – Optical Beam-Riding

OCC – Obus à Charge Creusé

OCOKA – Observation and fields of fire, Cover and concealment, Obstacles, Key terrain, and Avenues of Approach.

OCSW – Objective Crew-Served Weapon

OCU – Operational Centre Unit

ODE – Ordnance Development and Engineering (Singapore)

OEG – Occluded Eye Gun sight

OEO – optical and electro-optical

OFSA – Objective Family of Small Arms

OFSA – One Size Fits All

OFW – Objective Force Warrior

OHWS – Offensive Hand Weapon System

OIC – Officer in Charge

OICW – Objective Individual Combat Weapon

OOTW – Operations Other Than War

OP – Observation post

OP – Operators Panel

OPCON – Operational Control

OPDW – Objective Personal Defense Weapon

OPORD – Operations Order

OPSEC – Operational Security

OPV – Observation Post Vehicle

OSW – Objective Sniper Weapon

OSS (USAF) – Operational Support Squadron

OSW (USAF) – Operational Support, Weather

OT – operational test

OTA – over flight top attack

OTEA – Operational Test and Evaluation Agency (US)

P

P – How pack howitzer

P3I – Pre-Planned Product Improvements

PAR – pulse acquisition radar

PAT – power-assisted traverse

PC – Personal Computer

PCB – printed circuit board

PCC – Police Compact Carbine

PCI – Pre-combat inspection

PD – Point Defense

PD – point detonating

PD – Point of Departure

PDNA – Positioning Determining/Navigation Unit

PDRR – Program Definition and Risk Reduction

PDW – Personal Defence Weapon

PE – MoD Procurement Executive (UK)

PE – Peace Enforcement (US DoD)

PEC – Printed Electronic Circuits

PFD – proximity fuze disconnector

PFHE – prefragmented high explosive

PFPX – prefragmented proximity fuzzed

PGMM – Precision Guided Mortar Munitions

PH – Probability of Hit

Pi – Probability of incapacitation

PIAT – Projector, Infantry, Anti Tank

PIBD – Point Initiating Base Detonated

PID – Positive Identification

PIE – pyrotechnically initiated explosive

PIP – Product Improvement Programme

PL – Phase Line

PLA – People's Liberation Army

PLARS – Position Location And Reporting System (US)

PLC – Programmable Logic Control

PLO – Palestinian Liberation Army

PLOS – Predicted Line Of Sight

PLS – Palletised Load System (US)

PM – Porte mortier

PM – Product Manager

PMCS – Preventative Maintenance Checks and Services

PMEE – U.S. Air Force abbreviation for Prime Mission Electronic Equipment

PMO – Program Management Office (US)

PMO – Provost Marshall's Office

PMOD – Platform Modifications

PMS – Pedestal-Mounted Stinger

PNU - Position Navigation Unit

POA&M - Plan Of Action & Milestones

POF - Pakistan Ordnance Factory

POS - Postes Optiques de Surveillance

POW - Prisoner(s) of War

PPI - plan position indicator

PPS - Precise Positioning Service

PRAC - practice

PRAC-T - practice tracer

PRI - projector reticle image

PRP - Personnel Reliability Program

PSD - Propulsion System Demonstrator

PSO - Peace Support Operations

PSS - Primary Sight System

PTO - power take-off

PVP - Petit Véhicule Protégé

PW - Prisoner of War

PWI-SR (GR) - Panser Wagen Infanterie-Standaard (Groep)

PWP - Plasticized White Phosphorus

Q

QCB - Quick Change Barrel

QE - Quadrant Elevation

QRF - Quick Reaction Force

R

RA - Royal Artillery

RAAM - Rifle-launched Anti-Armour Munitions

RAAMS - Remote Anti-Armor Mine System (US)

PABD - Pay Entry Base Date

RAC - Royal Armoured Corps

RADIRS - Rapid Deployment Multiple Rocket System (US)

RAAF - Royal Australian Air Force

RAE - Royal Aircraft Establishment (Farnborough)

RAE - Royal Australian Engineers, Australian Combat Engineers

RAF - Royal Air Force

RAM-D - reliability, availability, maintainability and durability

RAN - Royal Australian Navy

RAO - Rear Area Operations

RAP - rocket-assisted projectile

RAPI - Reactive Armour Protection

RARDE - Royal Armament Research and Development Establishment (UK)

RATAC - Radar de Tir pour L'Artillerie de Campagne

RATELO - Radio Telephone Operator

RAW - Rifleman's Assault Weapon

RBL - Range and Bearing Launch

RC/MAS - Reserve Component/Modified Armament System

RCAAS – Remote-Controlled Anti-Armor System (US)

RCAF – Royal Canadian Air Force

RCC – ROLAND Coordination Center (US)

RCDU – Remote-Controlled Defence Unit

RCL – Recoilless rifle

RCN – Royal Canadian Navy

RCS – Radar Cross Section

RCT – Regimental Combat Team

RCT – Royal Corps of Transport

RCV – Robotic Command Vehicle

RDF – Rapid Deployment Forces

RDF/LT – Rapid Deployment Force Light Tank (US)

RDJTF – Rapid Deployment Joint Task Force (US)

RDT&E – Research Development Test and Evaluation

REME – Royal Electrical and Mechanical Engineers

RF – Rimfire

RFA – Royal Field Artillery

RFAS – Russian Federation and Associated States

RFC – Royal Flying Corps

RFI – request for information

RFP – request for proposals

RFPI – Rapid Force Projection Initiative

RFQ – Request For Quotations

RGGS – Rifle Grenade General Service

RHA – rolled homogeneous armour

RHA – Royal Horse Artillery

RIN – the former Royal Indian Navy

RIS – Rail Interface System

RISE – Reliability Improved Selected Equipment

RLC – Royal Logistic Corps

RLEM – Rifle-Launched Entry Munitions

RLG – Ring Laser Gyro

RLT – Regimental Landing Team

RMG – ranging machine gun

RN – Royal Navy

RNZAF – Royal New Zealand Air Force

RNZN – Royal New Zealand Navy

RO – Royal Ordnance

ROBAT – Robotic Counter-Obstacle Vehicle (US)

RoC – Republic of China

ROC – required operational characteristics

ROE – Rules Of Engagement

ROF – Royal Ordnance Factory (UK)

ROF – Rate Of Fire

RoK – Republic of Korea

RoKMC – Republic of Korea Marine Corps

RoKIT – Republic of Korea Indigenous Tank

ROR – range only radar

ROTA – Royal Ordnance Training Ammunition

RP – Red phosphorus

RP – rocket-propelled

RPC – Rocket Pod Container

RPG – Rocket-propelled grenade

RPG – Ruchnoy Protivotankovy Granatomyot

RPV – Remotely piloted vehicle

RR – Recoilless rifle

RRPR – Reduced Range Practice Rocket

RRTR – Reduced Range Training Round

RSAF – Royal Small Arms Factory (UK) (now closed)

RSS – Rosette Scanning Seeker

RTE – Rifle Team Equipment

RTT – Roues Transporteur de Troupes

RUC – Royal Ulster Constabulary

RWS – Remote weapon system (or station)

S

s – Second (s)

S&W – Smith & Wesson

SABCA – Société Anonyme Belge de Constructions Aéronautiques

SABR – Selectable Assault Battle Rifle

SABS – Stabilizing Automatic Bomb Sight

SAC – Small Arms Collimator

SACLOS – Semi-Automatic Command to Line Of Sight

SADA – Standard Advanced Dewar Assembly

SADARM – Sense And Destroy Armor (US)

SADF – South African Defence Force

SAE – Society of Automotive Engineers

SAF – Small Arms Fire

SAFCS – Small Arms Fire Control System

SAFIRE – Surface-to-Air Fire

SAL – semi-active laser

SAM – surface-to-air missile

SAMM – Société d'Applications des Machines Motrices

SANDF – South African National Defence Force

SANG – Saudi Arabian National Guard

SAP – Semi-Armour-Piercing

SAPHEI – Semi-Armour-Piercing High Explosive Incendiary

SAPI – semi-armour-piercing incendiary

SAS-EAS – Sealed Authenticator System - Emergency Action Procedures

SASR – Special Application Sniper Rifle

SAT – Small Arms Trainer

SATCP – Système Anti-aérien à Très Courte Portée

SAVA – Standard Army Vectronics Architecture

SAW – Squad Automatic Weapon

SAWS – Squad Automatic Weapon System

SB – Short Barrel

SCORE – Stratified Charge Omnivorous Rotary Engine

SD – self-destruct (ion)

SEAL – Sea/Air/Land

SEALOCK – Search, Locate, and Communicate or Kill

SEATO – Southeast Asia Treaty Organisation

SEME – School of Electrical and Mechanical Engineering

SEN – shell extended range NORICUM

SEP – Soldier Enhancement Programme

SFCS – Simplified Fire-Control System

SFIM – Société de Fabrication d'Instrument de Mesure

SFIRR – solid fuel integral rocket/ramjet

SFM – Sensor Fuzed Munitions

SFMG – Sustained Fire Machine Gun

SFSW – Special Forces Support Weapon

SFW – Special Forces Weapon

SGTS – Second-Generation Tank Sight

SH/PRAC – squash head practice

SHORAD – Short-Range Air Defence System

shp – shaft horsepower

SIC – Second in Command

SICPS – Standard Integrated Command Post Systems

SINCGARS – Single Channel Ground/Air Radio System

SIP – System Improvement Plan/Programme

SIPS – Small Integrated Propulsion System

SJFN – Semi-Jacketed Flat Nose

SJHP – Semi-Jacketed Hollow Point

SKOT – Sredni Kolowy Opancerzny Transporter

SLAP – saboted light armor penetrator

SLAW – Shoulder-Launched Assault Weapon

SLEP – Service Life Extension Program (US)

SLR – Self-Loading Rifle

SLR – Super Low Recoil

SLWAGL – Super Light Weight Automatic Grenade Launcher

SM – smoke

SMAW – Shoulder-launched Multi-purpose Assault Weapon

SMG – sub-machine gun

SMK – Smoke

Smoke – BE smoke base ejection

Smoke – WP smoke white phosphorus

SMP – Surface Mine Plough

SNAFU – Situation Normal, All Fouled Up

SNCO – Staff Non-Commissioned Officer

SNCOIC – Staff Non-Commissioned Officer in Charge (USMC)

SOCOM – Special Operations Command

SOF – Special Operations Force(s)

SOG – Speed over Ground

SOP – Standing/Standard Operational Procedure(s)

SP – Shore Patrol

SP – self-propelled

SP – Soft Point

SPAAG – self-propelled anti-aircraft gun

SPAAM – self-propelled anti-aircraft missile

SPAG – self-propelled assault gun

SPARK – solid propellant advanced ramjet kinetic energy missile

SPAS – Special Purpose Automatic Shotgun

SPATG – self-propelled anti-tank gun

SPAW – self-propelled artillery weapon

SPG – self-propelled gun

SPH – self-propelled howitzer

SPL – self-propelled launcher

SPLL – Self-propelled Loader Launcher

SPM – self-propelled mortar

SPP – Special Purpose Pistol

SPR – Special Purpose Rifle

SPS – Standard Positioning Service

SPSM – Sensorgezundete Panzerabwehr SubMunition

SPW – Special Purpose Weapon

SR – Short Rifle

SR – Staff Requirement

SRAW – Short Range Assault Weapon

SRC – Space Research Corporation

SRG – shell replenishment gear

SRI – Short Range Insert

SRTS – Short Range Thermal Sight

SRU – Shop Replaceable Unit

SRU – Slip Ring Unit

SRV – Surrogate Research Vehicle (US)

SSA – Special Spaced Armour

SSG – Single Shot Gun

SSK – Single Shot Kill

SSW – Squad Support Weapon

ST – Staff Target

STA – shell transfer arm

STAB – Steered Agile Beams

STAFF – Small Target Activated Fire-and-Forget (US)

STANAG - Standardization Agreement

STARTLE - Surveillance and Target Acquisition Radar for Tank Location and Engagement (US)

STE/ICE - Simplified Test Equipment/Internal Combustion Engine (US)

STOVL - Short Take Off and Vertical Landing

STUP - spinning tubular projectile

SUB - Substitute

SUC - Square Ultra Compact

SUIT - Sight Unit Infantry Trilux

SUSAT - Sight Unit Small Arms Trilux

SWARM - Stabilized Weapon and Reconnaissance Mount

SWAT - Special Weapons and Tactics

SWC - Semi Wad Cutter

SWS - Sniper Weapon System

T

T - Tracer

TACBE - Tacbe

TACMS - Army Tactical Missile System (US)

TACOM - Tank-automotive and Armaments Command (US)

TAD - Temporary Additional Duty (Naval Services term) Temporary Duty

TADDS - Target Alert Display Data Set (US)

TADS - Target Acquisition and Designation System (US)

TAM - Tanque Argentino Mediano

TAS - Target Acquisition Subsystem

TAS - tracking adjunct system

TAS - Turret Attitude Sensor

TBAT - TOW/Bushmaster Armored Turret (US)

TC - Tank Commander, also Truck Commander (US Army)

TCO - Tactical Combat Operations

TCTO - Time-Compliance Technical Order

TCU - tactical control unit

TD - Tank Destroyer

TDCS - Tank Driver Command System

TDD - Target Detection Device

TDR - Target Data Receiver

TDY - Temporary Duty

TE - Tangent Elevation

TEL - Transporter-Erector-Launcher

TELAR - Transporter-Erector-Launcher And Radar

TES - Tactical Environment Simulation

TES - target engagement system

TGMTS - Tank Gunnery Missile Tracking System

TGP - Terminally Guided Projectile

TGP - Targeting pod

TGS - Tank Gun Sight

TGSM - terminally guided SubMunition

TGTS - tank gunnery training simulator

TI - thermal imaging/imager

TIC - Troops in Contact

TICM - thermal imaging common modules

TIIPS - Thermal Imaging and Integrated Position System

TIM - Thermal Imaging Module

TIPU - Thermal Image Processing Units

TIRE - Tank Infra-Red Elbow

TIS - thermal imaging system

TLC - Transport Launching Container

TLD - Top Level Demonstrations

TLE - Treaty Limited Equipment

TLP -. Troop Leading Procedures (US)

TLR - Tank Laser Rangefinder

TLS - Tank Laser Sight

TM&LS - Textron Marine & Land Systems

TMBC - Turret Management Ballistic Computer

TMP - Tactical Machine Pistol

TMS - Turret Modernization System

TMUAS - Turreted Mortar Under Armor System (US)

TNT - Trinitrotoluene

TO - Technical Order

TOE - table of organization and equipment

TOGS - Thermal Observation and Gunnery System (UK)

TOP - Total Obscuring Power

TOPAS - Transporter Obrneny Pasovy

TOTE - Tracker, Optical Thermally Enhanced

TOW - Tube-launched, Optically tracked, Wire command link guided (US)

TP - Target Practice

TP-FL - target practice flash

TP-S - or TPS Target Practice-Spotting/Signature

TP-SM - target practice - smoke

TP-SP - target practice - spotting

TP-T - target practice - tracer

TPCM - Target Practice Colour-Marking

TPDS - Target Practice Discarding Sabot

TPFSDS-T - target practice fin-stabilized discarding sabot - tracer

TPTF - Target Practice Time Fuzed

TR - Triple Rail

TRACER - Tactical Reconnaissance Armoured Combat Equipment Requirement (UK)

TRACKSTAR - Tracked Search and Target Acquisition Radar System (US)

TRADOC - Training and Doctrine Command (US)

TSFCS - Tank Simplified Fire-Control System

TSQ - time and super-quick

TSR - Tavor Sporting Rifle

TT - transport de troupes (troop transporter)

TTB - Tank TestBed (US)

TTD - Transformation Technology Demonstrator

TTG - Time To Go

TTS - Tank Thermal Sight

TU - Terminal Unit

TU - Traversing Unit

TUA - TOW Under Armor (US)

TUR - Tiefflieger-Überwachungs-Radar (low-level surveillance radar)

TV - Television

TWD - Thermal Warning Device

TWMP - Track Width Mine Plough

TWS - Thermal Weapon Sight

TYDP - Ten Year Defence Programme (Australia)

U

UAV - Unmanned Aerial Vehicle

UBLE - Universal Bridge Launching Equipment

UCVP - Universal Combat Vehicle Platform

UDR - Ulster Defence Regiment

UET - Universal Engineer Tractor (US)

UGV - Unmanned Ground Vehicle

ULC - Unit Load Container

UMA - Universal Mounting Adapter

UMP - Universal Machine Pistol

USA - United States of America/United States Army

USAADS - U.S. Army Air Defense School

USAARMS - U.S. Army Armor School

USAAVNS - U.S. Army Aviation School

USAAF - United States Army Air Forces

USAF - United States Air Force

USCG - United States Coast Guard

USMC - United States Marine Corps

USN - United States Navy

USP - Universal Self-loading Pistol

UTL – Universal Tactical Light

UTM – Universal Transverse Mercator

UTS – Universal Turret System

UV – Ultraviolet

UW – Urban Warfare

V

V – Volt(s)

VAB – Véhicule de l'Avant Blindé (front armoured car)

VAB – Vickers Armoured Bridgelayer

VADS – Vulcan Air Defense System (US)

VAE – Vehiculo Armado Exploracion

VAK – Vehicle Adaptor Kit

VAPE – Vehiculo Apoyo y Exploracion

VARRV – Vickers Armoured Repair and Recovery Vehicle

VARV – Vickers Armoured Recovery Vehicle

VBC – Véhicule Blindé de Combat (armoured combat vehicle)

VBCI – Véhicule Blindé de Combat d'Infantrie

VBL – Véhicule Blindé Léger

VBM – Véhicules Blindés Modulaires

VC – Vehicle Commander

VCA – Véhicule Chenillé d'Accompagnement (tracked support vehicle)

VCC – Veicolo Corazzato de Combattimento

VCG – Véhicule de Combat du Genie

VCI – Véhicule de Combat d'Infantrie; Vehiculo combate infanteria

VCP – Vehicle Check Point

VCR – variable compression ratio

VCR – Véhicule de Combat à Roues

VCR/AT – Véhicule de Combat à Roues/Atelier Technique

VCR/IS – Véhicule de Combat à Roues/Intervention Sanitaire (stretchers)

VCR/PC – Véhicule de Combat à Roues/Poste de Commandement (HQ)

VCR/TH – Véhicule de Combat à Roues/Tourelle HOT

VCR/TT – Véhicule de Combat à Roues/Transport de Troupes

VCTIS -- Vehicle Command and Tactical Information System

VCTM – Vehiculo de Combate Transporte de Mortero

VCTP – Vehiculo de Combate Transporte de Personal

VDA – Véhicule de Défense Anti-aérienne

VDAA – Véhicule d'Auto-Défense Anti-aérienne

VDC – Voltage Direct Current

VDM – viscous damped mount

VDSL – Vickers Defence Systems Ltd

VDU – visual display unit

VEC – Vehiculo de Exploraciòn de Caballerie

VEDES – Vehicle Exhaust Dust Ejection System (US)

VERDI – Vehicle Electronics Research Defence Initiative (UK)

VHIS – visual hit indicator system

VIB – Véhicule d'Intervention du Base

VIDS – Vehicle Integrated Defence System

VINACS – Vehicle Integrated Navigation and Command System

VIRSS – Visual and InfraRed Smoke Screening System

VITS – Video Image Tracking Systems

VLAP – Velocity-enhanced Long-range Artillery Projectile

VLC – Véhicule Léger de Combat (light armoured car)

VLI – Visible Light Illuminator

VLSMS – Vehicle-Launched Scatterable Mine System

VMA – Marine Light Attack Squadron

VMA(AW) – Marine All-Weather Attack Squadron

VMBT – Vickers Main Battle Tank

VMF – Marine Fighter Squadron

VMFA – Marine Fighter Attack Squadron

VMFA(AW) – Marine All-Weather Fighter Attack Squadron

VMGR – Marine Aerial Refueler/Transport Squadron

VMFP – Marine Aerial Reconnaissance Squadron

VMR – Marine Transport Squadron

VMAQ – Marine Electronic Warfare Attack Squadron

VMS – Vehicle Motion Sensor

VNAS – Vehicle Navigation Air System

VRL – Véhicule Reconnaissance Léger

VSEL – Vickers Shipbuilding and Engineering Ltd

VT – variable time

VTOL – Vertical Take-Off and Landing aircraft

VTP – Véhicule transport de personnel

VTT – Véhicule transport de troupe

VVSS – vertical volute spring suspension

VXB – Véhicule Blindé à Vocations Multiples

W

WAAC – Women's Auxiliary Army Corps and individual members of; obsolete

WAC - Women's Army Corps and individual members of; obsolete

WAF - Women (in the) Air Force and individual members of; obsolete

WAM - Wide Area Mines (US)

WAMI - Wide Area Motion Imagery (US)

WAPC - Wheeled Armoured Personnel Carrier (Canada)

WASAD - Wide Angle Surveillance and Automatic Detection Device

WAV - Wide Angle Viewing

WAVES - Women Accepted for Volunteer Emergency Service (USN)

WES - Wing Engineer Squadron (USMC)

WFOV - Wide Field of View

WFSV - Wheeled Fire Support Vehicle (Canada)

WHA - Weapons Head Assembly

WHSA - Weapons Head Support Assembly

WLR - Weapon Locating Radar

WM - Woman/Women Marine(s)

WMD - Weapon(s) of Mass Destruction

WMRV - Wheeled Maintenance and Recovery Vehicle (Canada)

WP - white phosphorus

WP-T - white phosphorus - tracer

WSM - Winchester Short Magnum

WTS - Wing Transportation Squadron (USMC)

SECTION THREE

ABBREVIATIONS - GENERAL

GLOSSARY: LIST OF TERMS AND ACRONYMS

AA&E - Arms, Ammunition and Explosives

AAH - Asaib al-Haq

AAR - After Action Report

ACC - Accelerated Case Closure

ACDA- Arms Control and Disarmament Agency

ACLU - American Civil Liberties Union

ACOTA - African Contingency Operations Training and Assistance

Acpo - Association of Chief Police Officers

ACSA - Acquisition and Cross-Servicing Agreement

ADCMO - Assistant Deputy Chief Management Officer

ADL - Advanced Distance Learning

ADM- Administration and Management (DSCA Business Operations)

ADP- Automated Data Processing

ADP - Advanced Defense Policy

ADUSD(TP)- Assistant Deputy Under Secretary of Defense - Transportation Policy

AECA - Arms Export Control Act

AFI - Air Force Instruction

AFJMAN- Air Force Joint Manual

AFP - Annual Funding Plan

AFP - American Free Press

AFR-Africa Region

AFSAC-Air Force Security Assistance Center

AFSAT-Air Force Security Assistance Training

AGE-Aerospace Ground Equipment

AIAI-al-Itihad al-Islamyah - Somalia

AIG-Address Information Group

AIK-Assistance-in-Kind

AK Party-Justice and Development Party

ALCON-All Concerned

ALP-Aviation Leadership Program

AMC-Air Mobility Command

AMISOM-African Union Mission in Somalia

AMRAAM-Advanced Medium-Range Air-to-Air Missiles

AMSI-African Maritime Security Initiative

ANA-Afghan National Army

ANFO-Ammonium Nitrate-Fuel Oil

AoA-Analysis of Alternatives

AOR-Area of Responsibility

API-Application Programming Interface

APO-Army Post Office

APOD-Aerial Port of Debarkation

APOE-Aerial Port of Embarkation

APP-Associated Press of Pakistan

AQAP-Al-Qaeda in the Arabian Peninsula - Yemen

AQI-Al-Qa'idah-in-Iraq

AQIM-Algerian-based al-Qaeda in the Islamic Maghreb

AQLIM-Al-Qa'ida in the Lands of the Islamic Maghreb

AR-American Republic Region

AR-Army Regulation

ASD(APSA)-Assistant Secretary of Defense for Asian and Pacific Security Affairs

ASD(GSA)-Assistant Secretary of Defense for Global Security Affairs

ASD(HD&ASA)-Assistant Secretary of Defense for Homeland Defense and Americas' Security Affairs

ASD(ISA)-Assistant Secretary of Defense for International Security Affairs

ASD(ISP)-Assistant Secretary of Defense for International Security Policy

ASD(LA)-Assistant Secretary of Defense for Legislative Affairs

ASD(NII)-Assistant Secretary of Defense for Networks and Information Integration

ASD(RA)-Assistant Secretary of Defense for Reserve Affairs

ASD(SO/LIC)-Assistant Secretary of Defense for Special Operations/Low Intensity Conflict

ASD(SO/LIC-CN)-Assistant Secretary of Defense for Special Operations/Low Intensity Conflict/Counter-Narcotics

ASDA-Automated State Department Approval

ASG-Abu Sayyaf Group - Philippines

ASTQB-American Software Testing Qualifications Board

AT-Anti-Tamper

ATC-Anti-Terrorism Court

ATEA- Anti-Tamper Executive Agent

ATFP-Anti-Terrorism Assistance Programme

ATMG-Arms Transfer Management Group

ATPU-Anti-Terrorism Police Unit - Kenya

AV-Asset visibility

B2R-Budget-to-Report

BATFE-Bureau of Alcohol, Tobacco, Firearms, and Explosives

BEQ-Bachelor Enlisted Quarters

BOQ-Bachelor Officers' Quarters

BOS-Base Operating Support

BPR-Business Process Reengineering

BSC-Basilan State College

BSF-Border Security Force

BTA-Business Transformation Agency

C&A-Certification and Accreditation

C-SEAP-Cadet Semester Exchange Abroad Program

C4ISR-Command Control Communications Computers Intelligence Surveillance and Reconnaissance

CAA-Controlled Access Areas

CAAF-Court of Criminal Appeals for the Armed Forces

CACOL-USMC Center for Advanced Operational Culture Learning

CAIR-The Council on American-Islamic Relations

CAL-Category Assignment List

CAO-Collateral Action Officer

CAOCL-Center for Advanced Operational Culture Learning

CAPSOC-Commander Croatian Army Peace Support Operations Center

CAR-Central African Republic

CAS-Contract Administration Services

CBA-Commercial Banking Account

CBJ-Congressional Budget Justification

CBL-Commercial Bill of Lading

CBRN-chemical, biological radiological and nuclear weapons

CBS-Commercial Buying Service

CBSR-Census Bureau Shipment Report

CBT-Computer Based Training

CCB-Configuration Control Board

CCB-Bolivarian Continental Coordinating Board

CCBL-Collect Commercial Bill of Lading

CCIF-Combatant Command Initiative Fund

CCIMF-CENTCOM Commanders' International Military Fellows program

CCL-Coalition Chat Line

CCMR-Center for Civil Military Relations

CDM-Case Development Module

CDTS-Counter-Drug Training Support

CE-Central Command

CEMIS-Case Execution Management Information System

CEP-Civil Emergency Planning

CERI-Centre for International Studies Research - France

CERI-Centre for International Studies Research - France

CETS-Contractor Engineering Technical Services

CFD-Country Finance Director

CFLCC-Coalition Forces Land Component Command

CFM-Country Financial Management (DSCA Business Operations)

CFS-Contract Field Services

CHP-Republican People's Party - Turkey

CIA-Central Intelligence Agency

CIF-Cost, Insurance and Freight

CIO-Chief Information Officer

CIRA-Continuity IRA

CISIL-Centralized Integrated System for International Logistics

CJCS-Chairman of the Joint Chiefs of Staff

CJCSI-Chairman of the Joint Chiefs of Staff Instruction

CLAMO-Center for Law and Military Operations

CLOTP-Comprehensive Legal Officer Training Plan

CLSSA-Cooperative Logistics Supply Support Arrangement

CMC-Crisis Management Committee

CMEP-Civil-Military Emergency Preparedness

CMMOC-Romania's Crisis Management and Multinational Operations College

CMP-Comptroller (DSCA Business Operations)

CNDP-Congress National pour la Defense du People

COCOM-Combatant Command

CODEL-Congressional or Congressional Staff Delegation

COE-DMHA-The Center for Excellence in Disaster Management and Humanitarian Assistance

COESPU-Center of Excellence for Stability Police Units Vicenza, Italy

COI-Communities of Interest

COI's-Critical Operational Issues

COM-Chief of Mission (U.S. Diplomatic Mission)

COMSEC-Communications Security

CONUS-Continental United States

CONUSA-Continental United States Army

COP-Communities of Practice

COR-Contracting Officer's Representative

CORCOM-EDA Coordinating Committee

CPD-Country Program Director

CPI-Critical Program Information

CPI-Continuous Process Improvement

CPI-M-Communist Party of India - Maoist Militants

CPJP-Convention of Patriots for Justice and Peace

CPOI-Global Peace Operations Initiative

CRA-Continuing Resolution Authority

CRPF-Central Reserve Police Force - Indian Kashmir

CRS-Congressional Research Service

CSIS-Center for Strategic and International Studies

CSIS-Canadian Security Intelligence Service

CSP-Concurrent Spare Parts

CST-Caribbean Support Tender

CT-Counter Terrorism

CTC-Counter Terrorism Committee

CTFP-Combating Terrorism Fellowship Program

CTIP-Combating Trafficking in Persons

CTR-Cooperative Threat Reduction

CTWG-Partnership for Peace Consortium's Combating Terrorism Working Group

CUI-Controlled Unclassified Information

DAR-Data-at-Rest

DAS-Administrative Department of Security

DASA DEC-Deputy Assistant Secretary of the Army for Defense Exports and Cooperation

DASD-Deputy Assistant Secretary of Defense

DASD-PS-Deputy Assistant Secretary of Defense-Partner Strategy

DBO-DSCA Directorate of Business Operations

DBR-Defense Resources Board

DCA-Defense Cooperation in Armaments

DCAA-Defense Contract Audit Agency

DCC-Direct Commercial Contracts

DCMA-Defense Contract Management Agency

DCS-Direct Commercial Sale

DDA-Designated Disclosure Authority

DELG- Defense Export Loan Guarantee

DELP- Defense English Language Program

DEPSECDEF-Deputy Secretary of Defense

DESC-Defense Energy Support Center

DFARS-Defense Federal Acquisition Regulation Supplement

DFAS-Defense Finance and Accounting Service

DGR-Designated Government Representative

DGSE-General Directorate for External Security - France

DIA-Defense Intelligence Agency

DIACAP-Defense Information Assurance Certification and Accreditation Process rules.

DIADS-DSCA IMET Allocation Database System

DIC-Defense Industrial Cooperation

DIFS-Defense Integrated Financial System

DIILS-Defense Institute of International Legal Studies

DIMO-Defense Institute of Medical Operations

DISA-Defense Information Systems Agency

DISAM-Defense Institute of Security Assistance Management

DISCO-Defense Industrial Security Clearance Office

DISP-Defense Industrial Security Program

DLA-Defense Logistics Agency

DLAI-Defense Logistics Agency Instruction

DLIELC-Defense Language Institute English Language Center

DLIS-Defense Logistics Information Service

DMS-Defense Message System

DoC-Department of Commerce

DoD-Department of Defense

DoDD-Department of Defense Directive

DoDFMR-Department of Defense Financial Management Regulation

DoDI-Department of Defense Instruction

DoDIG-Department of Defense Inspector General

DoS-Department of State

DoS (ISN/MTR)-Department of State, Bureau of International Security and Nonproliferation/ Office of Missile Threat Reduction

DoS (PM)-Department of State (Bureau of Political and Military Affairs)

DoS (PM/DDTC)-Department of State - Directorate of Defense Trade Controls

DoS (PM/RSAT)-Department of State - Office of Regional Security and Arms Transfer Policy

DoT-Department of Transportation

DPDS-Defense Property Disposal Service

DRMO-Defense Reutilization and Marketing Office

DRMS-Defense Reutilization and Marketing Service

DSADC-Defense Security Assistance Development Center

DSAMS-Defense Security Assistance Management System

DSAWG-DISN Security Accreditation Working Group

DSI-Department of Special Investigations

DSP-Democratic Left Party - Turkey

DSS-Defense Security Service

DT-Developer Test

DTC-Delivery Term Code

DTIM-Delivery Traffic Indication Message

DTP-Democratic Society Party - Turkey

DTRA-Defense Threat Reduction Agency

DTS-Defense Transportation System

DTSA-Defense Technology Security Administration

DTSI-Defense Trade Security Initiative

DUP-Democratic Unionist Party - Ireland

DUSD(PS)-Deputy Under Secretary of Defense (Policy Support)

DVOT-Distinguished Visitor Orientation Tours

DWCF-Defense Working Capital Fund

DX-Direct Exchange

E-IMET-Expanded International Military Education and Training

E.O.-Executive Order

EACC-Enhanced Accelerated Case Closure

EAP-East Asia and Pacific Region

ECHR-European Court and Human Rights

ECL-English Comprehension Level

EDA-Excess Defense Article

EEE-Emergency, Extraordinary Expenses

EEOC-United States Equal Employment Opportunity Commission

EIMET-Expanded International Education and Training

EIPC-Enhanced International Peacekeeping Capabilities

ELN-Army of National Liberation

ELT-English Language Training

ENDP-Exception to National Disclosure Policy

EOQ-Economic Order Quantity

EPG-European Participating Governments

EPR-Enterprise Resource Planning

ESF-Economic Support Fund

ESI-Enterprise Software Initiative

ETSS-Extended Training Service Specialist

EU-European Union

EUM-End-Use Monitoring

EUR-European Region

FAA-Foreign Assistance Act

FAC-Colombian Air Force

FAD-Force Activity Designator

FAI-Federazione Anarchia Informale militants - Italy

FAO-Foreign Area Officer

FAR-Federal Acquisition Regulation

FARC-Fuerzas Armadas Revolucionarias de Columbia

FARDC-Forces Armees de la Republique Democratique du Congo - Armed Forces of the Democratic Republic of Congo

FATA-Federally Administered Tribal Areas - Pakistan

FATS-Firearms Training Simulator

FAW-Financial Analysis Worksheet

FBI-Federal Bureau of Investigation

FDLR-Forces Democratique de Liberation du Rwanda

FDS-Foreign Disclosure System

FFB-Federal Financing Bank

FICS-FMS Integrated Control System

FID-Foreign Internal Defense

FM-Financial Management

FM-Field Manual

FMC-Full Mission Capable

FMCS-Foreign Military Construction Services

FMF-Foreign Military Financing

FMFIMET-Foreign Military Financing and International Military Education and Training Budge Web Tool

FMS-Foreign Military Sales

FMS ADMIN-Foreign Military Sales Administrative (Fund)

FMSCR-Foreign Military Sales Credit

FMSO-Foreign Military Sales Order

FOAF-Friend of a Friend

FOB-Free On Board

FOIA-Freedom of Information Act

FORDTIS-Foreign Disclosure and Technical Information System

FPG-Foreign Procurement Group

FPO-Fleet Post Office

FPS-Financial Policy and Support (DSCA Business Operations)

FRB-Federal Reserve Bank

FRS-Federal Reserve System

FSB-Russian FSB (Federal Security Service)

FSC-Federal Supply Classification

FSG-Federal Supply Group

FSN-Foreign Service National

FSP-Field Studies Program (formerly IP - Informational Program)

FTD-Field Training Detachment

FTE-Field Training Exchanges

FVS-Foreign Visit System

FYDP-Future Years Defense Program

FYPA-Fiscal Year Planning Assessment

GAFS-General Accounting and Financial System

GAO-General Accounting Office

GBL-Government Bill of Lading

GC-General Counsel

GDF-Guyana Defense Force

GEBAT-Government Excess Baggage Authorization Ticket

GEF-Guidance for Employment of the Force (US DoD national military strategy)

GEF-Global Environment Fund

GEOINT-Geospatial-Intelligence

GFE-Government Furnished Equipment

GFEBS-General Fund Enterprise Business System (US Army)

GFM-Government Furnished Materiel

GPOI-Global Peace Operations Initiative

GPRA-Government Performance & Results Act

GPS-PPS-Global Positioning System - Precise Positioning System

GRE-Graduate Record Examination

GSA-General Services Administration

GSOMIA-General Security of Military Information Agreements

GWOT-Global War on Terrorism

HA-Humanitarian Assistance

HA/MA-Humanitarian Assistance and Mine Action

HAC-House Appropriations Committee

HAO-Humanitarian Assistance Other

HAP-Humanitarian Assistance Program

HAP-EP-Humanitarian Assistance Program - Excess Property

HAPC-Humanitarian Assistance Policy Committee

HASC-House Armed Services Committee

HAZMAT-Hazardous Materiel

HCA-Humanitarian and Civic Assistance

HDR-Humanitarian Daily Rations

HIG-Hizb-i-Islami - Gulbuddin

HIRC-House International Relations Committee

HIV-Human Immunodeficiency Virus

HQCLAN-Headquarters DSCA Classified LAN

HQULAN-Headquarters DSCA Unclassified LAN

I-LOMO-International Law of Military Operations

I-MET-International Military Education and Training

IA-Information Assurance

IA-Implementing Agency

IAAFA-Inter-American Air Forces Academy, San Antonio, TX

IAEA-International Atomic Energy Agency

IAM-Information Assurance Manager

IAPTC-International Association Peacekeeping Training Center

IARA-Islamic American Relief Agency

IATA-International Air Transport Association

IAVA's-Information Assurance Vulnerability Alerts

IAW-In Accordance With

ICASS-International Cooperative Administrative Support Services

ICC-International Criminal Court

ICCPR-International Covenant on Civil and Political Rights

ICG-International Contact Group

ICP-Inventory Control Point

ICRC-International Committee of the Red Cross

ICU-Islamic Courts Union

IDF-Israel Defense Forces

IDPs-Internally-Displaced Persons

IDT-Inactive Duty Training

IEC-Afghan-run Independent Election commission

IED-Improvised Explosive Device

IEMP-International Engine Management Programs

IFOR-Implementation Forces

IFR-Instrument Flight Rules

IFRI-French Institute on International Relations

IGOS-International Government Organizations

IHD-Human Rights Association

IHL-International Humanitarian Law

IIHL-International Institute of Humanitarian Law

IJU-Islamic Jihad Union

ILCO-International Logistics Control Office

ILOMO-International Law of Military Operations

ILS-Integrated Logistics Support

IMATT-International Military Assistance Training Team

IMC-Internal Management Control

IMELDA-International Maritime Enlisted Leadership & Development Assistance Program

IMET-International Military Education and Training

IMF-International Monetary Fund

IMOC-International Maritime Officers Course

IMSO-International Military Student Officer

IMU-Islamic Movement of Uzbekistan

INCLE-International Narcotics Control and Law Enforcement

IOO-International Operations Officers

IP-Internet Protocol

IPL-Integrated Priority List

IPO-(Navy) International Programs Office

IPOA-International Peace Operation Association

IRG-Iranian Revolutionary Guard

IRGC-Iranian Revolution Guards Corps

IRRD-Issue Release and Receipt Documents

ISAF-International Security Assistance Force - NATO led

ISAN-International Security Assistance Network

ISI-Inter-Services Intelligence

ISPR-Inter-Services Public Relations (Armed Forces of Pakistan)

ISR-Industrial Security Regulation

ISTL-Integrated Standardized Training List

ISWOS-International Surface Warfare Officers School

IT-Information Technology

ITAR-International Traffic in Arms Regulations

ITO-Invitational Travel Orders

JAG-Judge Advocate General

JCET-Joint Combined Exchange Training

JCS-Joint Chiefs of Staff

JEM-Justice and Equality Movement

JFTR-Joint Federal Travel Regulations

JI-Jamaat-i-Islami

JKDDC-Joint Knowledge Development and Distribution Capability

JKO-Joint Knowledge Online

JLOC-Joint Logistics Operations Center

JMPAB-Joint Materiel Priorities and Allocation Board

JR-Joint Regulation

JRA-Japanese Red Army

JRTN-Jaysh Rijal al-Tariq al-Naqshabandi

JSAT-Joint Security Assistance Training (Regulation)

JSOC-United States Joint Special Operations Command

JSOU-Joint Special Operations University

JTR-Joint Travel Regulations

JTTF-Joint Terrorism Task Force

JVI-Joint Visual Inspection

KCK-Kurdish Democratic Confederation

KGK-Kongra Gel

KL-Bill-Kerry-Lugar bill

KML-Keyhole Markup Language

KVM-Keyboard, Video, Monitor

LAA-Limited Access Authorization

LAAPA-Legal Aspects of Accountability in Military and Public Agencies

LCC-Legal Aspects of Combating Corruption

LCC-Legal Aspects of Combating Corruption

LCHR-Law of Armed Conflict and Human Rights

LCT-Legal Aspects of Combating Terrorism

LDTT-Legal Development Training Team

LeT-Lashkar-e-Taiyiba - India terrorists

LIFG-Libyan Islamic Fighting Group

LLRC-Language Learning Resource Center

LO/CLO-Low Observable/ Counter Low Observable

LOA-Letter of Offer and Acceptance

LOA-Letter of Offer and Acceptance

LOAC-Law of Armed Conflict

LOAD-Letter of Offer and Acceptance Data

LoC-Line of Control

LOI-Letter of Intent

LOR-Letter of Request

LPA-Legislative and Public Affairs

LRA-Lord's Resistance Army

LRC-Logistics Readiness Center (Chairman of the Joint Chiefs of Staff)

LSC-Logistics Support Charge

LSE-Logistics Support Expense

LTD-Language Training Detachments

LTTE-Liberation of Tamil Tigers Elam

MANPADS-Man-Portable Air Defense System

MAP-Military Assistance Program

MAPAD-Military Assistance Program Address Directory

MAPEX-Military Assistance Program Excess

MAPOM-MAP-Owned Materiel

MARAD-Maritime Administration

MASFEX-Military Assistance Service Funded Excess

MASL-Military Articles and Sales List

MCA-Military Commissions Act

MCC-Model Criminal Code

MCCP-Model Criminal Code Procedure

MCM-Manual for Court-Martials

MDA-Missile Defense Agency

MDE-Major Defense Equipment

MEDEVAC-Medical Evacuation

MEJA-Military Extraterritorial Jurisdiction Act of 2000

MEND-Movement for the Emancipation of the Niger Delta

MERLN-Military Education Research Library Network

MET-Mobile Education Team

MFA-Ministry of Foreign Affairs

MFP-Major Force Program

MFR-Memorandum for Record

MGK-National Security Council - Turkey

MHP-Nationalist Movement Party - Turkey

MIA-Missing in Action

MILAP-Military Department Approval

MILDEP-Military Department

MILF-Moro Islamic Liberation Front - Philippines

MILOB-Military Observer

MILSTRIP-Military Standard Requisitioning and Issue Procedures

MIMEX-Major Item Material Excess

MIRR-Materiel Inspection and Receiving Report

MISIL-Management Information System for International Logistics

MISWG-Multinational Industrial Security Working Group

MLA-Manufacturing Licensing Agreements

MLDP-Military Law Development Program

MLEPA-Model Law Enforcement Powers Act

MMSC-Model Maritime Service Code

MNS-Mission Needs Statement

MOA-Memorandum of Agreement

MOD-Ministry of Defense

MOU-Memorandum of Understanding

MPA-Military Personnel Account

MPAC-Muslim Public Affairs Council

MPIL-Max Planck Institute for Comparative Public Law and International Law - Heidelberg

MPP-Mission Performance Plan

MREs-Meals-Ready-to-Eat

MRI-MILSTRIP Routing Identifier

MS-Mission Sustainment

MSC-Military Sealift Command

MSI-DN-Italian Social Movement-National Right party

MTCR-Misile Technology Control Regime

MTDS-Manpower and Travel Data Sheet

MTT-Mobile Training Team

MUC-Multi user chat

NACSI-National Communication Security Instruction

NAD-National Armaments Director

NADR-Nonproliferation, Anti-Terrorism, Demining, and Related Programs

NAMSA-NATO Maintenance and Supply Agency

NATO-North Atlantic Treaty Organization

NAVICP-Naval Inventory Control Point

NAVINST-Navy Instruction

NAVSCIATTS-Naval Small Craft Instruction and Technical Training School, Stennis Space Center,

NC-Nonrecurring Cost

NCB-National Codification Bureau

NCIS-Naval Criminal Investigative Services

NCO-non-commissioned officer

NCP-National Congress Party - Sudan

NDAA-National Defense Authorization Act FY2010

NDP-National Disclosure Policy

NDPC-National Disclosure Policy Committee

NDPS-National Disclosure Policy System

NDU-National Defense University

NETSAFA-Naval Education and Training Security Assistance Field Activity

NFE-Non-Federal Entity

NGA-National Geospatial-Intelligence Agency

NGO-Non-Government Organization

NIE-United States National Intelligence Estimate

NIIN-National Item Identification Number

NIPO-Navy International Programs Office

NISP-National Industrial Security Program

NISPOM-National Industrial Security Program Operating Manual

NIST-National Institute of Standards and Technology

NJP-Nonjudical Punishment

NJS-Naval Justice School

NLFT-National Liberation Front of Tripura

NO-Northern Command

NOA-Notice of Availability

NOSC-Navy Operational Support Center

NPA-New People's Army - Philippines

NPA-New People's Army Philippines militants

NPS-Naval Post Graduate School

NR-Non Regional

NSA-National Security Agency

NSAS-National Security Assistance Strategy

NSC-National Security Council

NSD-National Security Directorate

NSDD-National Security Decision Directive

NSN-National Stock Number

NSSC-Notice of Supply and/or Service Completion

NTCIUP-Non-Traditional Communities of Interest and Unanticipated Partners.

NVD-Night Vision Device

NWFP-North West Frontier Province (in reference to Pakistan's Swat Valley area)

NYSPSA-New York State Political Science Association

O&M-Operations and Maintenance

O2C-Order-to-Cash

OA-Obligational Authority

OBL-Ocean Bill of Lading

OC-ALC-Oklahoma Air Logistics Center

OCCSG/HMA-Policy Coordinating Committee Subgroup on Humanitarian Mine Action

OCONUS-Outside the Continental United States

ODC-Office of Defense Cooperation

ODS-Ozone Depleting Substance

OED-Offer Expiration Date

OFDA-Office of Foreign Disaster Assistance

OGC-DSCA Office of General Counsel

OHDACA-Overseas Humanitarian, Disaster and Civic Air

OIF-Operation Iraqi Freedom

OIPT-NSPS Overarching Integrated Product Team

OJT-On-The-Job Training

OMB-Office of Management and Budget

OPI-Oral Proficiency Interviews

OPM-Organisasi Papua Merdeka

OPR-Office of Primary Responsibility

OPSEC-Operations Security

ORC-Offer Release Code

ORD-Operational Requirements Document

ORF-Official Representation Funds

ORT-Organization for the Renewal of the Temple - Jerusalem

OSCE-Organization for Security and Co-Operation in Europe

OSD-Office of the Secretary of Defense

OSP-Offshore Procurement

OT-Orientation Tour

OT-Operational Testing

OT&E-Operational Test and Evaluation

OTD-Operational Test Director

OTRR-Operational Test Readiness Review

P&A-Price and Availability

P2P-Procure-to-Pay

PA-Procurement Appropriation

PAO-Public Affairs Officer

PBAS-Program Budget Allotment System

PC&H-Packing, Crating, and Handling

PCC-Policy Coordinating Committee

PCH&T-Packing, Crating, Handling, and Transportation

PCR-Post-Conflict Reconstruction

PCS-Permanent Change of Station

PCSOs-Police Community Support Officers

PD-Presidential Determination

PDLI-Project Directive Line Item

PDM-Program Decision Memorandum

PEC-Pricing Element Code

PEM-Program Element Monitor

PFLP-Popular Front for the Liberation of Palestine

PFP-Partnership for Peace

PJAK-Iranian Affiliate the Free Life Party of Kurdistan Terrorist Organization

PKK-Partiya Karkaren Kurdistan militants - Turkey

PKK-Kurdistan Workers' Party - Turkey

PKLD-Peacekeeping: Latest Developments

PKO-Peace Keeping Operations

PKRL-Conducting Stability and Peacekeeping Operations in Accordance with the Rule of Law

PLAD-Plain Language Address Designator

PLAN-People's Liberation Army Navy

PM-Program Manager

PM/RSAT-Bureau of Political-Military Affairs/Office of Regional Security and Arms Transfers

PME-Professional Military Education

PML-Program Management Line

PMO-Program Management Office

PnP-Ports and Protocols

POC-Point of Contact

POD-Port of Debarkation

POE-Port of Embarkation

POM-Program Objective Memorandum

POTUS-President of the United States

POW-Prisoner of War

PPBS-Planning, Programming, and Budgeting System

PPP-Pakistan People's Party

PPR-Positions of Prominence Report

PPR-Pre-Planned Responses

PROS-Parts and Repair Ordering System

PSNI-Police Service of Northern Ireland

PSO-Peace Support Operations

PTI-Press Trust of India

PWS-Performance Work Statement

QAT-Quality Assurance Team

QIC-Quick Intervention Corps

QOL-Quality of Life

R&D-Research and Development

RAM-Random Access Memory

RAM-Random Antiterrorism Measure

RAW-[Indian Intelligence Agency, (Research and Analysis Wing)]

RCMP-Royal Canadian Mounted Police

RCN-Record Control Number

RCS-Reports Control Symbol

RDF-Resource Description Framework

RDT&E-Research, Development, Test & Evaluation

RFP-Request for Proposal

RIM-Retainable Instructional Materials

RIO-Regional International Outreach

RIPs-Rapid Improvement Projects

RM-Resource Management

ROE-Rules of Engagement

ROZs-Reconstruction Opportunity Zones

RPD-Regional Program Director

RRN-Ready Responders Network

RSI-Rationalization, Standardization, and Interoperability

RSLAF-Republic of Sierra Leone Armed Forces

RULOPS-Rules of Law and Disciplined Military Operations

SA-Security Assistance

SAAM-Special Assignment Airlift Mission

SAARMS-Security Assistance Automated Resource Management Suite

SAC-Senate Appropriations Committee

SAF/IA-Secretary of the Air Force for International Affairs

SAMM-Security Assistance Management Manual

SAN-Security Assistance Network

SANG-Saudi Arabia National Guard

SAO-Security Assistance Organization/Officer

SAPRWG-Security Assistance Planning and Review Working Group

SAS-Special Air Service

SASC-Senate Armed Services Committee

SAT-Security Assistance Team

SATFA-Security Assistance Training Field Activity

SBA-Special Billing Arrangement

SBLC-Standby Letter of Credit

SC-Serious Crimes

SCES-Security Cooperation Enterprise Solution

SCETC-Security Cooperation Education and Training Center

SCETWG-Security Cooperation Education and Training Working Group

SCHOLAR-SPAWAR Collaboration Hub and Online Learning Architecture

SCI-Special Compartmented Information

SCIF-Sensitive Compartmented Information Facility

SCIP-Security Cooperation Information Portal

SCMS-Security Cooperation Management Suite

SCO-Security Cooperation Office

SCO-Tweb-Security Cooperation Office - Training web

SDAF-Special Defense Acquisition Fund

SDDC-(Military) Surface Deployment and Distribution Command

SDI-Strategic Defense Initiative

SDP-Strategy and Defense Policy

SDR-Supply Discrepancy Report

SECDEF-Secretary of Defense

SECSTATE-Secretary of State

SED-Shipper's Export Declaration

SET-Specialized English Training

SFOR-Stabilization Force

SFRC-Senate Foreign Relations Committee

SHAPE-Supreme Headquarters Allied Powers, Europe

Shin Bet-Israel Security Agency

SIA-Security Industry Authority

SIMILIE-Semantic Interoperability of Metadata and Information in unlike Environments (MIT Project)

SL-Sendero Luminoso Militants - Peru

SLA-Sri Lankan Army

SLM/A-Sudan Liberation Movement/Army

SLN-Sri Lanka Navy

SMART-Specific, Measureable, Actionable, Relevant, Timely - Lean Six Sigma acronym

SME-Subject Matter Expert

SME-Significant Military Equipment

SMS-Short Message Service (for cell phones)

SNAP-Simplified Nonstandard Acquisition Process

SO/LIC-Special Operations/ Low Intensity Conflict

SOCO-DoD Standards of Conduct Office

SOF-Special Operations Forces

SOFA-Status of Forces Agreement

SOP-Standard Operating Procedure

SORN-System of Record Notice

SOW-Statement of Work

SPAN-DoD Security Policy Automation Network

SPLA-Sudan People's Liberation Army

SPLC-The Southern Poverty Law Centre

SPNB-Statecraft, Peacekeeping and Nation Building

SPO-Systems Program Office

SR-Specialized English Training Required

SROE-Standing Rules of Engagement

SSA-Security Sector Assistance

SSR-Security Sector Reform

SSR-LAP-Security Sector Reform Legal Assistance Program

SSS-Selective Service System

STIG-DISA Security Technical Implementation Guide

STL-Standardized Training List

SVBIED-Suicide Vehicle-Borne Improvised Explosive Device

SVI-Single Vendor Integrity

SVP-Swiss People's Party

SWIFT-The Society for Worldwide Interbank Financial Telecommunications

SWOS-Surface Warfare Officers School

TAA-Technical Assistance Agreement

TAC-Type of Address Code

TAD-Temporary Additional Duty

TAFT-Technical Assistance Field Team

TAR-Team After-Action Review

TAT-Technical Assistance Team

TBC-Transportation Bill Code

TCCP-Transitional Code of Criminal Procedure

TCG-Technical Coordinating Group

TCI-Terrorism and Counter-insurgency

TCK-Turkish Penal Code

TCN-Transportation Control Number

TDA-Transitional Detention Act

TDP-Technical Data Package

TDR-Transportation Discrepancy Report

TDY-Temporary Duty

TECOM-Training and Education Command

TFG-Somalia's Transitional Federal Government

TI DAC-Transparency International Defense Against Corruption

TL-Termination Liability

TL-Test Leads

TLA-Travel and Living Allowance

TLK-Tactical Language Kits

TLW-Termination Liability Worksheet

TM-Training Module

TMS-Training Management System

TOBB-Turkish Union of Chambers and Commodity Exchanges

TOC-Table of Contents

TOEFL-Test of English as a Foreign Language

TOR-Term of Reference

TOW-2B-Tube-Launched, Optically-Tracked, Wire-Guided Missile

TPA-Total Package Approach

TPMR-Training Program Management Review

TPS-Technology Protection System

TR-Trouble Reports

TRADOC-Training and Doctrine Command Armed Forces of the Republic of Albania

TRANSCOM-U.S. Transportation Command

TRT-Turkish Radio and Television Corporation

TTP-Tehrik-i-Taliban Pakistan

UCL-University College London

UCMJ-Uniform Code of Military Justice

UDC-Union Democratique de Centre

UFR-Unfunded Requirement

UFR-Union des Forces de la Résistance

ULFA-United Liberation Front of Assam

ULFA-United Liberation Front of Assam - Minarets

ULO-Unliquidated Obligation

UMMIPS-Uniform Material Movement and Issue Priority System

UN-United Nations

UND-Urgency of Need Designator

UNESCO-United Nations Educational, Scientific and Cultural Organization

UNHRC-United Nations High Commissioner for Refugees

UNLOA-United Nations Letters of Assist

UNPD-United Nations Police Division

UNPOL-United Nations Police

UNSG-United Nations Secretary General

UNTSO-United Nations Truce Serpersion Organization

UPT-Undergraduate Pilot Training

URL-Uniform Resource Locator - Internet

USAF-United States Air Force

USAID-(United States) Agency for International Development

USAK-International Strategic Research Organization

USAMMA-United States Army Medical Materiel Agency

USARCS-United States Army Claims Service

USAREUR-United States Army - Europe

USARPAC-United States Army - Pacific

USASAC-United States Army Security Assistance Command

USC-United States Code

USCENTCOM-United States Central Command

USCG-United States Coast Guard

USD(AT&L)-Under Secretary of Defense for Acquisition, Technology, and Logistics

USD(C)-Under Secretary of Defense, Comptroller

USD(I)-Under Secretary of Defense for Intelligence

USD(P)-Under Secretary of Defense for Policy

USDR-United States Defense Representative

USEUCOM-United States European Command

USG-United States Government

USIP-United States Institute of Peace

USJFCOM-United States Joint Forces Command

USMC-United States Marine Corps

USN-United States Navy

USPACOM-United States Pacific Command

VBIED-Vehicle-Borne Improvised Explosive Device

VFR-Visual Flight Rules

VMS-Vulnerability Management System

VOA-Serbian Military Intelligence Agency

VRAE-Valley of the Rivers Apurimac and Energy - Peru

VTC-Video Teleconferencing

WAAS-Washington Headquarters Services Allotment Accounting System

WCF-Working Capital Fund

WCN-Worksheet Control Number

WFP-United Nations World Food Programme

WHINSEC-Western Hemisphere Institute for Security Cooperation

WHS-Washington Headquarters Services

WIF-Warsaw Initiative Fund

WMD-Weapons of Mass Destruction

WPAFB-Wright - Patterson Air Force Base - Ohio

WPOD-Water Port of Debarkation

WPOE-Water Port of Embarkation

WSLO-Weapons System Logistics Officer

XMPP-Extensible Messaging and Presence Protocol

YSML-United States Munitions List

ABBREVIATIONS-GENERAL II

A

ABM: Anti Ballistic Missiles

ABVP: Akhil Bharatiya Vidyarthi Parishad

AC: Alternating Current; Ashoka Chakra

ACU: Asian Currency Union

AD: anno Domini; in the year of Lord Christ

ADB: Asian Development Bank

ADC: Aide-de-Camp; Access Deficit Charge

ADF: Asian Development Fund

ADS: Air Defence Ship

AJT: Advanced Jet Trainer

AG: Accountant General; Adjutant General

AI: Air India

AIDS: Acquired Immune Deficiency Syndrome

AIIMS: All India Institute of Medical Sciences

AIR: All India Radio; Annual Information Report

AITUC: All India Trade Union Congress

ALH: Advanced Light Helicopter

AM: ante meridiem; before noon

AMC: Army Medical Corps; Asset Management Companies

AME: Associate Member of the Institute of Engineers

APC: Agricultural Prices Commission

APEC: Asia-Pacific Economic Cooperation

APPLE: Ariane Passenger Payload Experiment

APPU: Asian Pacific Postal Union

ARC: Asset Reconstruction Company

ARDR: Agricultural and Rural Debt Relief

ASAT: Anti-Satellite weapon

ASC: Army Service Corps

ASCI: Advanced Strategic Computing Initiative

ASCII: American Standard Code for Information

ASEAN: Association of South-East Asian Nations

ASEM: Asia-Europe Meeting

ASIMO: Advanced Step in Innovative Mobility

ASLV: Augmented Satellite Launch Vehicle

ASMA: Antarctica Specially Managed Area

ASSOCHAM: Associated Chambers of Commerce and Industry

ATA: Air Time Authority; Allen Telescope Array

ATC: Air Traffic Controller

ATM: Automatic Teller Machine

ATR: Action Taken Report

ATV: Automatic Transfer Vehicle

AUM: Assets Under Management

AVC: Army Veterinary Corps

AVM: Additional Volatility Margin

AWACS: Airborne Warning and Control System

B

BARC: Bhabha Atomic Research Centre

BBC: British Broadcasting Corporation

BC: Before Christ; Board of Control; Battery Commander

BCG: Bacillus Calmette Guerin

BICP: Bureau of Industrial Costs and Prices

BIFR: Board of Industrial and Financial Reconstruction

BIOS: Basic Input Output System

BKU: Bharatiya Kisan Union

BMD: Ballistic Missile Defence System

BOLT: BSE On-Line Trading (System)

BOSS: Bharat Operating System Solutions

BPO: Business Process Outsourcing

BPR: Bottom Pressure Records

BRO: Border Road Organisation

BSE: Bombay Stock Exchange

BSF: Border Security Force

BSNL: Bharat Sanchar Nigam Ltd

C

CA: Chartered Accountant

CABE: Central Advisory Board of Education

C & AG: Comptroller & Auditor General

CAIR: Centre for Artificial Intelligence and Robotics

CAPART: Council for People's Action and Advancement of Rural Technology

CAPES: Computer-Aided Paperless Examination System

CAS: Chief of Army Staff; Chief of Air Staff; Conditional Access System

CB: Citizen Band (Radio)

CBI: Central Bureau of Investigation

CBFC: Central Board of Film Certification

CCPA: Cabinet Committee on Political Affairs

CD: Conference on Disarmament

C-DAC: The Centre for Development of Advanced Computing

CDMA: Code Division Multiple Access

CECA: Comprehensive Economic Cooperation Agreement

CERN: European Organisation for Nuclear Research

CFC: Chlorofluro Carbon

CFS: Container Freight Station

CHOGM: Commonwealth Heads of Government Meeting

CIA: Central Intelligence Agency

CIBIL: Credit Information Bureau (India) Ltd

CIC: Chief Information Commissioner

CID: Criminal Investigation Department

C-in-C: Commander-in-Chief

cif: cost, insurance and freight

CIS: Commonwealth of Independent States

CISF: Central Industrial Security Force

CITES: Convention on International Trade in Endangered Species

CITU: Centre of Indian Trade Unions

CLASS: Computer Literacy and Studies in Schools

CLAWS: Centre for Land Warfare Studies

CM: Command Module; Chief Minister

CMP: Common Minimum Programme

CNG: Compressed Natural Gas

CNN: Cable News Network

CNS: Chief of the Naval Staff

CO: Commanding Officer

COD: Central Ordnance Depot; Cash on Delivery

CPCB: Central Pollution Control Board

CPI: Communist Party of India

CPI(M): Communist Party of India (Marxists)

CPU: Central Processing Unit

CR: Central Railway

CRAC: Cyber Regulation Advisory Council

CRDI: Common Rail Direct injection

CRISIL: Credit Rating Information Services of India Limited

CRM: Customer Relationship Management

CRR: Cash Reserve Ratio

CRPF: Central Reserve Police Force

CSIR: Council of Scientific and Industrial Research

CTBT: Comprehensive Test Ban Treaty

CTT: Commodities Transaction Tax

CVRDE: Combat Vehicles Research and Development Establishment

D

DA: Dearness Allowance; Daily Allowance

DAVP: Directorate of Advertising and Visual Publicity

DC: Deputy Commissioner; Direct Current in Electricity

DDT: Dichloro-Diphenyl Trichloro-ethane

DIN: Director Information Number

DM: District Magistrate; Deputy Minister

DMIC: Delhi-Mumbai Industrial Corridor

DMK: Dravida Munnetra Kazhagam

DNA: de-oxyribonucleic acid

DO: Demi-official (letter)

DOD: Department of Ocean Development

DPEP: District Primary Education Programme

DPI: Director of Public Instruction

DRAM: Dynamic Random Access Memory

DRDO: Defence Research and Development Organisation

DST: Daylight Saving Time

DRES: Department of Renewable Energy Sources

DTH: Direct to Home (broadcasting)

E

ECG: Electro Cardio-gram

ECS: Electronic Clearing Service

ECT: Electro-convulsant Therapy

EDUSAT: Education Satellite

EEG: Electro-encephalography

EET: Exempt-2 Taxation

EFA: Education for All

EFF: Extended Fund Facility

e.g.: exempli gratia; for example

EHTP: Electronic Hardware Technology Parks

ELISA: Enzyme Linked Immuno Solvent Assay

EMI: Equated Monthly Installment

EMS: European Monetary System

EMU: Electric-Multiple Unit; Extra-vehicular Mobility Unit

E & OE: Errors and Omissions Excepted

EPROM: Erasable Programmable Read Only Memory

ER: Eastern Railway

NER: North Eastern Railway

ERM: Exchange Rate Mechanism

ERNET: Educational and Research Network

ESA: European Space Agency

ESCAP: Economic and Social Commission for Asia and the Pacific

ESMA: Essential Services Maintenance Act

ESOP: Employee Stock Option Programme

etc.: et cetera (and other things)

EU: European Union

EVM: Electronic Voting Machine

F

FAO: Food and Agriculture Organisation

FBI: Federal Bureau of Investigation

FCNR: Foreign Currency (non-resident) Accounts Scheme

FDR: Flight Data Recorder; Fixed Deposit Receipt

FEMA: Foreign Exchange Management Act

FERA: Foreign Exchange Regulations Act

FICCI: Federation of Indian Chambers of Commerce and Industry

FII: Foreign Institutional Investors

FIPB: Foreign Investment Promotion Board (of India)

FLAG: Fibre Optic Link Around the Globe

FM: Field Marshal; Frequency Modulated; Fiance Minister

FPSB: Financial Planning Standards Boards (India)

FRBM: Fiscal Responsibility and Budget Management

FSSA: Food Safety and Standards Authority (of India)

FTA: Free Trade Area

FTP: File Transfer Protocol

G

GAGAN: GPS-aided Geo-augmented Navigation

GAIL: Gas Authority of India Limited

GAIN: Global Alliance for Improved Nutrition

GATS: General Agreement on Trade in Services

GATT: General Agreement on Tariffs and Trade

GCA: General Currency Area

GCC: Gulf Cooperation Council

GCM: Greatest Common Measure

GEF: Global Environment Fund

GHQ: General Headquarters

GIC: General Insurance Corporation

GIST: Graphics and Intelligence-based Script Technology

GMPS: Global Mobile Personal Communications System

GMRT: Giant Meter wave Radio Telescope

GMT: Greenwich Mean Time

GNSS: Global Navigation Satellite System

GNP: Gross National Product

GOC: General Officer Commanding

GPO: General Post Office

GPRS: General Packet Radio System

GPS: Global Positioning System

GSLV: Geosynchronous Satellite Launch Vehicle

GSP: Generalized Special Preferences

GST: Goods and Service Tax

GSTP: Global System of Trade Preferences

H

HAWS: High Altitude Warfare School

HCF: Highest Common Factor

HDI: Human Development Index

HDTV: High Definition Television

HE: His (or Her) Excellency; His (or Her) Eminence; High Explosive; Horizontal Equivalent

HITS: Headend In The Sky

HMMWV: High Mobility Multipurpose-Wheeled Vehicle

HMS: Hybrid Mail Service

HP: Himachal Pradesh; Horizontal Plane; Horse Power

HTML: Hyper Text Markup Language

HTTP: Hypetext Transfer Protocol

HUDCO: Housing and Urban Development Corporation

HVDC: High Voltage Direct Current

I

IAAI: International Airport Authority of India

IAAS: Indian Audit and Accounts Service

IADF: International Agricultural Development Fund

IAEA: International Atomic Energy Agency

IAF: Indian Air Force

IAMC: Indian Army Medical Corps

IAS: Indian Administrative Service

IATA: International Air Transport Association

IATT: Inland Air Travel Tax

IBRD: International Bank for Reconstruction and Development

IBEX: Interstellar Boundary Explorer Mission

ICANN: Internet Corporation for Assigned Names and Numbers

ICAO: International Civil Aviation Organisation

ICAR: Indian Council of Agricultural Research

ICCR: Indian Council of Cultural Relations

ICCW: Indian Council for Child Welfare

ICDS: Integrated Child Development Service

ICJ: International Court of Justice

ICL: Indian Cricket League

ICMR: Indian Council of Medical Research

ICPA: Indian Cricket Players' Association

ICRC: International Committee of the Red Cross

IDA: International Development Association

IDBI: Industrial Development Bank of India

IDSA: Institute of Defence Studies and Analysis

i.e.: id est; that is

IEA: International Energy Agency

IES: Indian Economic Service

IEX: Indian Energy Exchange

IFRS: International Financial Reporting Standard

IFS: Indian Foreign Service; Indian Forest Service

IFTU: International Federation of Trade Unions

IFWJ: Indian Federation of Working Journalists

IGNOU: Indira Gandhi National Open University

IIPA: Indian Institute of Public Administration

IISS: International Institute of Strategic Studies

IIT: Indian Institutes of Technology

ILO: International Labour Organisation

IMA: Indian Military Academy

IMET: International Military Education Training Programme

IMF: International Monetary Fund

IMO: International Maritime Organisation

IN: Indian Navy; Intelligent Network

INA: Indian National Army

INK: International Newspaper Kiosks

INMARSAT: International Maritime Satellite Organisation

INMAS: Institute of Nuclear Medicines and Allied Sciences

INS: Indian Naval Ship; Indian Newspaper Society

INSAS: Indian Small Arms System

INSAT: Indian National Satellite

INTERPOL: International Police Organisation

INTUC: Indian National Trade Union Congress

IOC: International Olympic Committee

IP: Indian Police

IPC: Indian Penal Code

IPCC: Intergovernmental Panel on Climate Change

IPEC: International Programme on Elimination of Child Labour

IPR: Intellectual Property Right

IPS: Indian Police Service; Indian Postal Service

IPTV: Internet Protocol Television

IPU: Inter-Parliamentary Union

IQ: Intelligence Quotient

IR: Infra-red

IRA: Insurance Regulatory Authority

IRBM: Intermediate Range Ballistic Missile

IREP: Integrated Rural Energy Planning

IRS: Indian Remote Sensing Satellite; Indian Revenue Service

ISAF: International Stabilization and Assistance Force

ISC: Inter-State Council

ISCS: Integrated Smart Card System

ISD: International Subscriber Dialled

ISH: Information Super Highway

ISKCON: International Society for Krishna Consciousness

ISO: International Standardization Organisation

ISP: Internet Service Provider

ISRO: Indian Space Research Organisation

ISS: International Space Station

IST: Indian Standard Time

ISTRAC: ISRO Telemetry, Tracking and Command Network

ITDC: Indian Tourism Development Corporation

ITO: International Trade Organisation; Income-tax Officer

ITU: International Tele-communication Union

IUC: Interconnect User Charge

J, K, L

JCO: Junior Commissioned Officer

JNNURM: Jawahar Lal Nehru National Urban Renewal Mission

JPC: Joint Parliamentary Committee

JPEG: Joint Photographic Experts Group

JWG: Joint Working Group

KG: Kindergarten

Kg: Kilogramme

KPO: Knowledge Process Outsourcing

LAC: Line of Actual Control

LCA: Light Combat Aircraft

LDC: Least Developed Countries

LHC: Large Hadron Collider

LIC: Life Insurance Corporation (of India)

LLP: Limited Liability Partnership

LOAC: Line of Actual Control

LTA: Light Transport Aircraft; Leave Travel Allowance

LTTE: Liberation Tigers of Tamil Eelam

M

MAT: Minimum Alternative Tax

MER: Mars Exploration Rover

MBBS: Bachelor of Medicine and Bachelor of Surgery

MCF: Master Control Facility

MEP: Minimum Export Price

MES: Military Engineering Service

METSAT: Meteorological Satellite

MFA: Multi-Fibre Agreement

MFN: Most Favoured Nation

MIP: Moon Impact Probe

MMS: Multimedia Messaging Service

MMTC: Minerals and Metals Trading Corporation of India

MNC: Multi-national Corporation

MNIC: Multi-purpose National Identity Card

MODEM: Modulator-Demodulator

MRI: Magnetic Resonance Imaging

MRTPC: Monopolies and Restrictive Trade Practices Commission

MRTS: Mass Rapid Transit System

MSA: Maritime Safety Agency

MSCF: Maritime Security Cooperation Framework

Mss: Manuscript

MTCR: Missile Technology Control Regime

MTO: Multilateral Trade Organisation

MVC: Maha Vir Chakra

MUNO: A large red dildo that sings and dances on the children's show, "I heard that dildo went into Sally clean and came out muno"

N

NAA: National Airport Authority

NABARD: National Bank for Agriculture and Rural Development.

NACIL: National Aviation Company of India Ltd

NADA: National Anti-Doping Agency

NAEP: National Adult Education Programme

NAFTA: North America Free Trade Agreement

NAG: National Air Guard

NAM: Non-aligned Movement

NAMA: Non-Agriculture Market Access

NASA: National Aeronautics and Space Administration

NASDAQ: National Association of Securities Dealers Automated Quotation

NATA: Natural Aptitude Test for Architecture

NATO: North Atlantic Treaty Organisation

NAV: Net Asset Value

NB: Nota bene; note well, or take notice

NCA: Nuclear Command Authority

NCC: National Cadet Corps

NCEP: National Committee on Environmental Planning

NCERT: National Council of Education Research and Training

NCR: National Capital Region

NDA: National Defence Academy; National Democratic Alliance

NDNC: National Do Not Call (Registry)

NDPS: Narcotic Drugs & Psychotropic Substances

NDRF: National Disaster Response Force

NDTL: National Dope Testing Laboratory

NeGP: National e-governance Plan

NEDB: North-Eastern Development Bank

NEP: National Education Policy

NEPA: National Environment Protection Authority

NFO: New Fund Offers

NHDP: National Highways Development Project

NHRC: National Human Rights Commission

NIC: National Integration Council

NIFT: National Institute of Fashion Technology

NIO: National Institute of Oceanography

NIS: National Institute of Sports

NIT: National Institute of Technology

NLMA: National Literacy Mission Authority

NMD: Nuclear Missile Defence

NMDC: National Mineral Development Corporation

NPL: National Physical Laboratory

NPR: National Population Register

NPT: (Nuclear) Non-Proliferation Treaty

NRBI: National Rural Bank of India

NREGA: National Rural Employment Guarantee Act

NREP: National Rural Employment Programme

NRF: National Renewal Fund

NRI: Non-Resident Indian

NRR: National Reproduction Rate

NRSA: National Remote Sensing Agency

NSA: National Security Act

NSC: National Service Corps; National Security Council

NSDL: National Securities Depository Limited

NSE: National Stock Exchange

NSR: National Skills Registry

NTPC: National Thermal Power Corporation

NWDA: National Water Development Agency

NWRC: National Water Resources Council

O

OAS: Organisation of American States

OAU: Organisation of African Unity

OBC: Other Backward Communities

OBU: Offshore Banking Unit

ODA: Official Development Assistance

ODF: Open Document Format

ODS: Ozone Depletion Substances

OECD: Organisation of Economic Co-operation and Development

OGL: Open General Licence

OIC: Organisation of Islamic Countries

OIGS: On India Government Service

OIL: Oil India Limited

OM: Order of Merit

ONGC: Oil and Natural Gas Commission

OPEC: Organisation of Petroleum Exporting Countries

OSCE: Organisation for Security and Cooperation in Europe

OSD: Officer on Special Duty

OXML: Open Extended Marking Language

P

PAC: Political Affairs Committee; Public Accounts Committee

PACER: Programme for Acceleration of Commercial Energy Research

PAN: Permanent Account Number (of Income-Tax)

PATA: Pacific-Asia Travel Association

PCS: Public Civil Service; Punjab Civil Service

PIB: Press Information Bureau

Pin Code: Postal Index Number Code

PIO: Persons of Indian Origin

PLF: Plant Load Factor

PM: Post Meridiem; after-noon; also Postmaster; Prime Minister;

PMG: Postmaster General

PN: Participatory Note

PO: Post Office; Postal Order

POPs: Persistent Organic Pollutants; Point of Purchase

POTA: Prevention of Terrorism Act

POW: Prisoner of War

PP: Public Prosecutor; Particular Person

PRO: Public Relations Officer

PS: Post Scriptum; Post Script; written after

PSC: Public Service Commission

PSE: Public Sector Enterprises

PSLV: Polar Satellite Launch Vehicle

PTA: Preferential Trade Area

PTI: Press Trust of India

PTO: Please Turn Over; Privilege Ticket Order

PUFA: Poly Unsaturated Fatty Acids

PVC: Param Vir Chakra

PVSM: Param Vishisht Sewa Medal

PWD: Public Works Department

Q, R

QMG: Quarter Master General

QR: Quantitative Restriction

RAF: Rapid Action Force

RAM: Random Access Memory

RBI: Reserve Bank of India

RCC: Reinforced Concrete Cement

RDF: Rapid Development Force

RDS: Radio Data Servicing

RDSS: Radio Determination Satellite Service

REACH: Rehabilitate, Educate and Support Street Children

RLO: Returned Letter Office

RLV: Reusable Launch Vehicle

RPM: Revolution Per Minute

RPO: Recruitment Process Outsourcing; Regional Passport Officer

RRB: Regional Rural Bank

RRPI: Rural Retail Price Index

RSS: Rashtriya Swayamsevak Sangh

RSVP: Repondez s'il vous plait (Fr.) reply, if you please

RTGS: Real Time Gross Settlement System

S

SAARC: South Asian Association for Regional Co-operation

SAFTA: South Asian Free Trade Area

SAIL: Steel Authority of India Limited

SAPTA: SAARC Preferential Trading Agreement

SARS: Severe Acute Respiratory Syndrome

SATNAV: Satellite Navigation (Initiative)

SAVE: SAARC Audio Visual Exchange

SC: Security Council; Supreme Court; Scheduled Caste

SCI: Shipping Corporation of India

SCO: Shanghai Cooperation Organisation

SCOPE: Standing Conference on Public Enterprises

SDO: Sub-Divisional Officer

SDR: Special Drawing Rights (created by the World Bank)

SEBI: Securities and Exchange Board of India

SFC: Strategic Forces Command

SGPC: Shiromani Gurudwara Prabandhak Committee

SIDBI: Small Industries Development Bank of India

SIT: Special Investigation Team

SITE: Satellite Instructional Television Experiment

SLR: Statutory Liquidity Ratio

SMS: Short Messaging Service; Subscriber Management System

SOS: Save Our Souls – distress signal

SPG: Special Protection Group

SPIN: Software Process Improvement Networks

SPV: Solar Photo Voltaic

SQUID: Super-conducting Quantum Interference Device

SRE: Space Capsule Recovery Experiment

SRV: Submarine Rescue Vessel

SSN: Social Security Number

STARS: Satellite Tracking and Ranging Station

START: Strategic Arms Reduction Talks

STEP: Science and Technology Entrepreneurship Park

STT: Securities Transaction Tax

SWAN: State-wide Area Network

SWIFT: Society for Worldwide Financial Telecommunications

T

TA: Travelling Allowance; Territorial Army

TAAI: Travel Agents Association of India

TACDE: Tactics and Air Combat Development Establishment

TADA: Terrorist and Disruptive Activities (Prevention) Act

TAPS: Tarapur Atomic Power Station

TB: Tuberculosis

TDC: Transport Development Council

TDS: Tax Deduction at Source

TDSAT: Telecom Dispute Settlement Appellate Tribunal

TERLS: Thumba Equatorial Rocket Launching Station

TIFR: Tata Institute of Fundamental Research

TIN: Tax Information Network

TINXSYS: Tax Information Exchange System

TISCO: Tata Iron and Steel Company

TMC: Terrain Mapping Camera

TMO: Telegraphic Money Order

TNT: Tri-nitro-toluene (high explosive)

TPP: 20-Point Programme

TRAI: Telecom Regulatory Authority of India

TRIMs: Trade Related Investment Measures

TRIPS: Trade Related Intellectual Property Rights

TRP: Television Rating Points; Tax Return Preparer

TRYSEM: Training of Rural Youth for Self Employment

TTE: Travelling Ticket Examiner

TTF: Tourism Task Force

U

UAE: United Arab Emirates

UAV: Unmanned Aerial Vehicle

UF: United Front

UFO: Unidentified Flying Object

UGC: University Grants Commission

ULFA: United Liberation Front of Assam

UN: United Nations

UNCTAD: United Nations Conference on Trade and Development

UNDP: United Nations Development Programme

UNEF: United Nations Emergency Force

UNEP: United Nations Environment Programme

UNESCO: United Nations Educational, Scientific and Cultural Organisation

UNFPO: United Nations Fund for Population Activities

UNHCR: United Nations High Commissioner for Refugees

UNHRC: United Nations Human Rights Commission

UNI: United News of India

UNICEF: United Nations International Children's (Emergency) Fund

UNIDO: United Nations Industrial Development Organisation

UNRRA: United Nations Relief and Rehabilitation Administration

UNTAC: United Nations Transitional Authority for Cambodia

UPA: United Progressive Alliance

UPSC: Union Public Service Commission

UPTN: Universal Personal Telephone Number

USA: United States of America

USIS: United States Information Service

V

VAT: Value-added Tax

VC: Vice-Chancellor; Vice Counsel; Victoria Cross; Vir Chakra

VDIS: Voluntary Disclosure of Income Scheme

VHRR: Very High Resolution Radiometer

VIP: Very Important Person

VLSI: Very Large Scale Integration

VOIP: Voice Over Internet Protocol

VPN: Virtual Private Network

VPP: Value Payable Post

VRS: Voluntary Retirement Scheme

VSAT: Very Small Aperture Terminals

W

WADA: World Anti-Doping Agency

WAP: Wireless Application Protocol

WAVE: Wireless Access for Virtual Enterprise

WDF: Wasteland Development Force

WEF: World Economic Forum

WFP: World Food Programme

WFTU: World Federation of Trade Unions

WGIG: Working Group on Internet Governance

WIPO: World Intellectual Property Organisation

WLL: Wireless in Local Loop

WMD: Weapons of Mass Destruction

WR: Western Railway

WTO: World Trade Organization (previously called GATT); also World Tourism Organization

X, Y, Z

XML: Extensible Markup Language

YMCA: Young Men's Christian Association

YWCA: Young Women's Christian Association

SECTION FOUR

Disposal of Medals- Instructions, Distributions and Forfeiture

Regulations 676 to 726

Extract

CHAPTER XVI

MEDALS AND DECORATIONS

676. Grant and Issue of Medals and Ribbons: (a) The institution of medal and decoration will be published in Gazette of India and also notified through Army Instructions. Medals will be obtained from the Medal Section, Ministry of Defence and ribbons for medals from the respective ordnance establishments but such demands will not be made until the publication of necessary authority in the Gazette of India/Army Instructions, (b) Instructions for issue and disposal of medals for gallantry awards will be contained in the AO/AI published at the time. Claims in respect of personnel on active service will be initiated by Record Offices only after they are posted to peace stations. Medals and decorations prescribed by the Central Government to be presented by high dignitaries to the awardees will not be issued.

677. Permission to Wear Medal Ribbons: When the grant of a medal has been notified and the medal rolls submitted to the Medals Section, OsC may authorise all ranks whose names are entered in the rolls to wear the ribbon. Ribbons for medals will be obtained free on demand from the respective ordnance establishments, but such demands will not be made until the publication of necessary authority in the Gazette of India/Army Instructions.

678. Method of Wearing Ribbons And Medals: Instructions regarding the method of wearing ribbons and medals are contained in Dress Regulations. For the orders of precedence for wearing the various decorations and medals, see para 717.

679. Recommendations for Gallantry Awards: Recommendations for gallantry awards and mention in despatches will be submitted to the Military Secretary, Army Headquarters through proper channels in accordance with IAFZ-3046. In no case will any indication be given to the individual concerned or to a person not directly concerned in an official capacity that a recommendation for an award has been made to a higher authority.

680. Publications of Awards of Gallantry Decorations: The names of those persons upon, or on account of, whom, a decoration may be conferred by the President will be published in the Gazette of India together with full citations for the Param Vir Chakra and Ashoka Chakra and brief citations for the remaining awards. These awards will thereupon be notified through Army Orders and Unit Orders.

681. Presentation of Medals and Decorations: (a) The procedure for Presentation of Medals and decorations will be as follows:

(i) Param Vir Chakra and Ashoka Chakra will be presented by the President immediately before the Republic Day Parade on 26 Jan. Along with decoration, a scroll signed by the President setting out the deed or deeds of valour will be presented to the recipient (or next of kin for posthumous award).

(ii) Other decorations namely the Param Vishisht Seva Medal, the Mahavir Chakra, the Kirti Chakra, the Ati Vishisht Seva Medal, the Vir Chakra, the Shaurya Chakra will be presented by the President at a formal Investiture annually. When a recipient/next of kin is unable to attend the President's Investiture the decoration will be sent by post. In special cases the President may present the decoration informally.

(b) The Sena/Nao Sena/Vayu Sena medals and Vishisht Seva Medals will be presented by the respective service Chiefs at a Presentation Parade to be decided by the Service Headquarters. Other services medals and decorations will whenever possible be presented to the recipient on Parade with befitting ceremony.

682. Safe Custody of Medals: (a) An officer receiving medals for issue will arrange for their safe custody.

(b) When medals are presented to individuals, receipts will be obtained from the recipients and such receipts as are required to be returned to the Medal Section, Ministry of Defence will be sent to that authority.

683. Safe Custody of Medals While Engaged in Active Operations: Medals and decorations will not be taken into active operations. All ranks, including reservists rejoining the colours on mobilization, who have any medals and decorations in their possession at the time of proceeding to active operations will be asked, if they so desire to place their medals in safe custody with the O i/c Records. The O i/c Records will be furnished with nominal and descriptive lists of such individuals who deposit their medals in the Record Office.

Those who do not deposit their medals for safe custody with the O i/c Records will be required to sign a certificate to the effect that they are neither taking their medals in active operations nor depositing them in the Record Office, to prevent any claims being made on their return from active operations or on demobilization.

684. Safe Custody of Medals on Board Transports: On board transports when troops are proceeding to, or returning from abroad, all medals and decorations of officers, JCOs, WOs, OR or NCs(E) will be handed over to the OC troops for safe custody during the voyage.

685. Storage of Medals: Medals will never be placed in store, attached to uniform.

686. Disposal of Medals of Individuals Illegally Absent: Medals left behind by an individual who absents himself without leave and is declared by a court of inquiry to be illegally absent will be forwarded to the Medal Section, Ministry of Defence. Such medals will be reclaimed should the absentee rejoin from absence.

687. Disposal of Medals on Transfer of Awardees: Medals received for individuals who have been transferred to other units will be transmitted to the OsC units concerned.

688. Disposal of Medals of Persons of Unsound Mind: Medals of persons who become insane and are subsequently removed from active list or discharged from service, will be made over to their claimants/heirs along with the individuals' other personal effects, If there is no such claimant/heir traceable, the provisions of para 690 will apply.

689. Disposal of Medals of Ex-Servicemen: Medals/Stars other than Gold/Silver Medals of ex-servicemen including retired officers will be sent to them direct by Officers Commanding Units/ record offices by registered post Acknowledgement due. Gold/ Silver Medals will be sent to the recipients by registered and insured post. In all cases acknowledgements duly receipted by ex-servicemen, received from the postal authorities, will be retained.

690. Disposal of Medals of Deceased Personnel: Medals and decorations of deceased personnel, whose next of kin are not traceable, will remain in the custody of the Medal Section, Ministry of Defence. Such medals may however be disposed of in accordance with the provisions of para 691 (c).

691. Disposal of Medals on Death in Service: The medals of an officer, JCO, WO, OR or NC (E) dying in service, whether issued before or after his death, will be disposed of as follows:

(a) If there is a will, the medals will be sent to the person who, in the opinion of the committee of adjustment/OC unit is named in the will as being intended to receive them or any articles that would, in their opinion, include them or as being a general or residuary legatee of the estate.

(b) In default of and subject to any such testamentary disposition, the medals will be sent to the widow/widower or next of kin in the following order of relationship—eldest surviving son or grandson, eldest surviving daughter or daughter's son, father, mother, eldest surviving brother or sister.

(c) In the case of a universal or residuary bequest to more than one person either in common or jointly, or when medals cannot be disposed as in (a) or (b) above, they may be sent to any relative or other interested party e.g., unit regimental centre, municipality/ village committee of the deceased who, in the opinion of the committee of adjustment/Officer i/c Records, will preserve them with due care as a memorial to the deceased.

692. Param Vir Chakra: This decoration is awarded for most conspicuous bravery, or some daring or pre-eminent act of valour or self-sacrifice in the presence of enemy, whether on land, at sea, or in the air. It ranks first among all the gallantry awards. Acts of gallantry entitling a person, to PVC on subsequent occasions are recognized with the award of a bar to the decoration for each such occasion. Posthumous awards can be made. Monetary allowance for PVC is shown in P & A Regs. Persons eligible for the decoration are:

(a) Officers, JCOs, WOs, OR and NCs(E) and women of all ranks of the Army, of any of the Reserve Forces, of the Territorial Army, Militia, and of any other lawfully constituted Armed Forces.

(b) Matrons, Sisters, Nurses and the staff of the Nursing Services and other services pertaining to Hospitals and Nursing, and civilians of either sex serving regularly or temporarily under the orders, directions or supervision of any of the above mentioned forces.

693. Maha-Vir Chakra: This decoration is awardable for acts of gallantry in the presence of the enemy whether on land, at sea, or in the air. Acts of gallantry entitling a person to MVC on subsequent occasions are recognized with the award of a bar to the decoration for each such occasion. Posthumous awards can be made. Monetary allowance for MVC is shown in P & A Regs. Categories of persons eligible for this decoration are the same as for PVC shown in para 692.

694. Vir Chakra: This decoration is awardable for acts of gallantry in the presence of the enemy, whether on land, at sea or in the air. Acts of gallantry entitling a person to Vr C on subsequent occasions are recognized with the award of a bar to the decoration for each such occasion. Posthumous awards can be made. Monetary allowance for Vr C is shown in P & A Regs. Categories of persons eligible for this decoration are the same as for PVC shown in para 692.

695. Ashoka Chakra Series: (a) Ashoka Chakra series of awards which consist of the Ashoka Chakra, Kirti Chakra and Shaurya Chakra, are awarded for acts of gallantry, as under, otherwise than in the face of the enemy:

(i) Ashoka Chakra. Awardable for most conspicuous bravery or some act of daring or pre-eminent valour or self-sacrifice.

(ii) Kirti Chakra. Awardable for conspicuous gallantry.

(iii) Shaurya Chakra. Awardable for gallantry.

(b) Persons eligible for the above decorations are:

(i) Officers and men and women of all ranks of the Army, of any of the reserve forces, of the Territorial Army, Militia and of any other lawfully constituted Forces;

(ii) Members of the Nursing Services of the Armed Forces;

(iii) Civilian citizens of either sex in all walks of life other than members of Police Forces and of recognized Fire Services.

The decorations may be awarded posthumously.

(c) Acts of gallantry entitling a person to any of the above decorations on subsequent occasions are recognized with the award of a Bar to that decoration for each such occasion. For every such Bar, a replica of the Chakra in miniature shall be added to the riband when worn alone.

(d) Monetary Allowance. Monetary allowance is shown in P and A Regs.

696. Vishisht Seva Medal Series: (a) Vishisht Seva Medal series are awarded for distinguished service as under:

(i) Param Vishisht Seva Medal. Awardable for distinguished service of the most exceptional order.

(ii) Ati Vishisht Seva Medal. Awardable for distinguished service of an exceptional order.

(iii) Vishisht Seva Medal. Awardable for distinguished service of a high order.

(b) Persons eligible for the medals are:

(i) Commissioned officers, JCOs, other ranks and non-combatants (enrolled) of the Regular Army, embodied auxiliary and reserve forces or any other lawfully constituted Army Forces;

(ii) Nursing officers and other members of Nursing Services in the Armed Forces.

The decorations may be awarded posthumously.

(c) If a recipient of the above mentioned medal(s) is subsequently awarded the same medal, for every such award he shall be given a Bar to be attached to the riband by which the medal is suspended. For every such Bar, miniature insignia of a pattern approved by Government shall be added to the riband when worn alone.

697. Sena Medal (Army Medal) and Vayu Sena Medal (Air Force Medal): (a) Sena Medal is awarded in recognition of such individual acts of exceptional devotion to duty or courage as have special significance for the Army. A bar shall be given for every subsequent award of the medal to a person.

(b) Persons eligible for the Sena Medal are:

(i) Commissioned officers, JCOs, other ranks and non-combatants (enrolled) of the Regular Army, embodied Auxiliary and Reserve Forces or any other lawfully constituted Armed Forces.

(ii) Nursing Officers and other members of Nursing Services in the Armed Forces.

(c) Vayu Sena Medal is given in recognition of such individual acts of exceptional devotion to duty or courage as have special significance for the Air Force. All ranks of Air Force and Army officers serving as pilots in Army Observation Post flights shall be eligible for the medal. The above awards may be made posthumously.

698. Sainya Seva Medal (Service Medal) With Clasps: (a) this medal is in recognition of non-operational service under difficult and trying conditions. It will have clasps Jammu & Kashmir, NEFA, Himalaya, Andaman and Nicobar and Bengal-Assam.

(b) Persons eligible for the award are:

(i) Commissioned Officers, JCOs, Other Ranks and Non Combatants (Enrolled) of the Regular Army, embodied Auxiliary and Reserve Forces or any other lawfully constituted Armed Forces.

(ii) Nursing Officers and other members of Nursing Services in the Armed Forces.

(c) A person who is awarded a gallantry decoration in the course of his service in any of the areas specified in sub paras (e), (f) and (g) below will be eligible for the award appropriate to the area irrespective of the time limit or the prescribed minimum number of sorties or flying hours.

(d) A person who dies on service or is evacuated as a result of wounds or other disabilities attributable to service in any of the areas specified in sub paras (e), (f) and (g) below will be eligible for the award appropriate to the area irrespective of the time limit or the prescribed minimum number of sorties or flying hours.

(e) Clasp Jammu & Kashmir:

(i) A person who has completed an aggregate of one year commencing from 27 October 1947 or thereafter on the effective strength of a unit/formation located within the geographical limits of the State of Jammu & Kashmir.

(ii) A member of the ejection crew of Air Despatch unit who has carried out a minimum of 10 sorties or 40 hours of flying commencing from 27 October 1947 and thereafter on transport support roles in the geographical limits of the State of Jammu & Kashmir.

(iii) A person who has earned Clasp Jammu & Kashmir to the General Service Medal 1947 will not count this service in that area prior to 1 January 1949 for the purpose of this award.

(f) Clasp NEFA:

(i) A person who has completed an aggregate of one year on the effective strength of a unit/formation located within the geographical limits of NEFA between the period of 7 October 1952 and 15 November 1958 and was employed on road/air field construction.

(ii) A person who has been seconded to Assam Rifles and has completed an aggregate service of one year in the geographical limits of NEFA commencing from 15 August 1947 or thereafter.

(iii) A member of the ejection crew of Air Despatch unit who has carried out a minimum of 10 sorties or 40 hours of flying on transport support roles in the geographical limits of NEFA commencing from 7 October 1952 or thereafter.

(g) Clasp Himalaya:

(i) A person who has been detailed for duties connected with the defence of the Northern Borders and who has completed an aggregate of one year on the effective strength of a unit /formation in the areas which will be specified from time to time by the Government.

(ii) A member of the ejection crew of Air Despatch unit who has carried out a minimum of 10 sorties or 40 hours of flying on transport support roles in the areas which will be specified from time to time by the Government.

(h) Clasp Andaman and Nicobar:

(i) A person who has completed an aggregate of one year service on the active strength of a unit/formation located in the geographical limits of Andaman and Nicobar from 20th May 56 or thereafter;

(ii) A member of the ejection crew of Air Despatch units and personnel borne on the effective strength of the Air Maintenance Battalion, Air Despatch Units and Air Observation Posts Units who have carried out a minimum of 10 sorties or 40 hours of flying commencing from 20th May 56 or thereafter on the transport support roles in the geographical limits of Andaman and Nicobar.

(b) Army units employed for the defence of the air-fields and directly supporting the operational units of the Air Force at Gauhati and Jorhat, e.g., HQ and units of RASO, Signals, ASC, DSC, and Artillery.

(c) MIZO HILLS district service in the area will count for the eligibility of Sainya Seva Medal with clasp 'BENGAL-ASSAM' from 1st Feb 64 to 27th Feb 66.

(d) Disturbed areas of Sibsagar and North Cachar districts South of the Line connecting Diphu Lumding.

WEST BENGAL

From 26th Oct 62 and onwards

Districts of Darjeeling, Jalpaiguri (including Siliguri and Cooch-Behar)

A member of the ejection crew of Air Despatch Units who has carried out a minimum of 10 sorties or 40 hours of flying on reconnaissance or transport/tactical support roles in the geographical limits of areas mentioned above.

(k) A person qualifying for the medal for the first time shall be awarded the Medal together with a Clasp. On subsequent occasions when the award is made, only a Clasp indicating the place where the service was rendered will be awarded.

699. Videsh Seva Medal (Overseas Medal) With Clasp:

(a) This medal is in recognition of service rendered outside the territories of the Union of India.

(b) Persons eligible for the award are:

(i) Commissioned Officers, JCOs, Other Ranks and Non-Combatants (Enrolled) of the Regular Army, embodied Auxiliary and Reserve Forces or any other lawfully constituted Armed Forces.

(ii) Nursing Officers and other members of Nursing Services in the Armed Forces.

(c) A person who is awarded a gallantry decoration in the course of his service in the countries specified in sub para(g) below will be eligible for the award appropriate to the area irrespective of the time limit or the prescribed minimum number of sorties or flying hours.

(d) A person who dies on service or is evacuated as a result of wounds or other disabilities attributable to service in the countries specified in sub para (g) below will be eligible for the award appropriate to the area irrespective of the time limit or the prescribed minimum number of sorties or flying hours.

(e) A person on the regular staff of a diplomatic mission in the countries specified in sub para (g) below does not fall within the purview of these provisions.

(f) The qualifying period for the award of the Medal shall not exceed the period of assignment. If the period of assignment is one year or more the qualifying period shall be 6 months. If the period of assignment is less than one year, the qualifying period shall be 3 months. In special cases, the period required for eligibility may be relaxed by the Government.

(g) (i) Clasp UAR: A person who has served for not less than 180 days continuously on the effective strength of the United Nations Emergency Force commencing from 2 November 1956 or thereafter.

(ii) Clasp Ethiopia: A person who has served for not less than 180 days on the staff of Haille Sellassie I Military Academy commencing from 3 May 1957, or thereafter.

(iii) Clasp Indo China: A person who has served for not less than 90 days continuously on the staff of the International Commission for Supervision and Control commencing from 7th August 1954 or thereafter.

(iv) Clasp Iraq: A person who has served for not less than 180 days continuously on deputation to the Government of Iraq from 10 November 1959 or thereafter.

(v) Clasp Korea: A person who has served for not less than 90 days continuously on the effective strength of the Neutral Nations Repatriation Commission or the Custodian Force, India between 22 November 1950 and 17 March 1954. A person who has received Clasp "Overseas Korea – 1950-53" to the General Service Medal 1947 will not be eligible for this award.

(vi) Clasp Lebanon: A person who has served for not less than 90 days on the effective strength of the United Nations Observer Group in Lebanon between 19 June 1958 and 12 December 1958.

(vii) Clasp Nepal: (aa) A person who has served for not less than

180 days continuously on the effective strength of a unit or formation employed on the construction of Tribunal Rajpath' and air fields in Nepal between 15 April 1952 and 15 April 1958.

(ab) A person who has served for not less than 90 days continuously and was employed on the provision of signal communication for the Government of Nepal, in Nepal between 26 November 1958 and 3 May 1959

(ac) A person who has served for not less than 180 days on the effective strength of the Indian Military Training Mission or the Indian Military Training Advisory Group in Nepal commencing from 1 August 1952 or thereafter.

(ad) A member of the ejection crew of Air Despatch unit who has carried out 6 sorties or 24 flying hours on transport support roles over Nepal commencing from 1 April 1952 or thereafter.

(viii) Clasp Congo:

(aa) A person who has served for not less than 180 days continuously on the effective strength of the UN Forces in CONGO commencing from 2 Aug 60 or thereafter.

(ab) A member of the ejection crew of the Air Despatch Units who has carried out 6 sorties or 24 hours of flying on transport support roles over Congo commencing from 2 Aug 60 or thereafter.

(ix) Clasp Bhutan:

(aa) A person who served on the effective strength of the Army team in Bhutan between 27 May 61 and 22 Sep 61

(ab) A person who has served for not less than 180 days continuously on the effective strength of the Indian Military Training Team in BHUTAN commencing from 27 Aug 62 or thereafter.

(ac) A person who has served for not less than 180 days continuously on the effective strength of a unit or formation employed on the construction of roads in BHUTAN commencing from 8 Apr 61 or thereafter.

(ad) A person on temporary duty in Bhutan, as may be specified by Government from time to time, for 90 days or more continuous service.

(ae) In the case of Air Observation Posts Pilots, 3 sorties or 12 flying hours if the period of assignment is less than one year and 6 sorties or 24 flying hours if the period of assignment is one year or more commenting from 8 April 61 or thereafter, on reconnaissance, or tactical transport roles over BHUTAN. In special cases the condition regarding the minimum number of sorties or flying hours may be relaxed by Government.

(x) Clasp Nigeria: A person who has served for not less than 180 days while on deputation to the Government of Nigeria commencing from 28 Dec 63 or thereafter.

(xi) Clasp Yemen; A person who has served on the staff of the United Nation Yemen Observation Mission between 4 Sep 63 and 4 Sep 64.

(xii) Clasp Bangladesh:

(aa) Personnel engaged in mine-sweeping operations in and around Bangladesh. The minimum qualifying service shall be 1 day in actual mine sweeping. The period of eligibility shall be from 26 Mar 72 to 30 Nov 72 (both days inclusive).

(ab) Personnel who participated in Chittagong Hills Operations on 26 Mar 72 or thereafter Minimum qualifying service shall be 1 day.

(xiii) Clasp Mauritius:

(aa) Personnel on deputation to the Government of Mauritius from 25 Feb 73 or thereafter

(ab) Service in Mauritius in connection with the restoration of power, and telecommunication network damaged due to cyclone in that country between 21 Feb 75 and 17 Jun 75.

(xiv) Clasp Afghanistan: Personnel on deputation to the Government of Afghanistan from 23 Jun 70 or thereafter.

(xv) Clasp Zambia: Personnel on deputation to the Government of Zabmia from 8 Oct 73 or thereafter.

(xvi) Clasp Ghana: Personnel on loan to the Government of Ghana commencing from 23 Mar 59 or thereafter.

(xvii) Clasp Sri Lanka:

(aa) Service on deputation to the Government of Sri Lanka or on loan to the Sri Lanka Navy commencing from the 13 Jun 60 or thereafter

(ab) A person who has served in Sri Lanka for a minimum period of two days during he period from 12 Apr to 25 May 71, and

(ac) A person who flew a minimum of 3 sorties or completed 3 hours of flying while on service in Sri Lanka during the period from 12 Apr to 25 May 71

(xviii) Clasp Sudan: Personnel on deputation to the Government of Sudan from 25 Nov 76 or thereafter.

(xix) Clasp Oman: Personnel on deputation to the Government of Sultan of Oman from Jun 67 or thereafter.

(xx) Clasp Botswana: Personnel on deputation to the Government of Botswana from 2 Aug 78 or thereafter.

(h) A person qualifying for the medal for the first time shall be awarded a medal together with a clasp. On subsequent occasions when the award is made, only a clasp indicating the place where the service was rendered will be awarded.

700. **Yudn Seva Medal Series:** (a) Yudh Seva Medal series of awards which consist of the Sarvottam Yudh Seva Medal, Uttam Yudh Seva Medal and Yudh Seva Medal are awarded, as under, for distinguished service during war/conflict/hostilities on or after 26th Jan 80:

(i) Sarvottam Yudh Seva Medal. Awardable for distinguished service of the most exceptional order.

(ii) Uttam Yudh Seva Medal. Awardable for distinguished service of art exceptional order.

(iii) Yudh Seva Medal. Awardable for distinguished service of a high order.

(b) Persons eligible for the above medals are:

(i) All ranks of the Army, the Navy and Air Force including those of Territorial Army Units, Auxiliary and Reserve Forces and other lawfully constituted Armed Forces when embodied.

(ii) Nursing Officers and other members of the Nursing Services in the Armed Forces.

The medals may be awarded posthumously:

(c) If a recipient of any of the above mentioned medals is subsequently awarded the same medal, every such further award shall be recognized by a Bar to be attached to the riband by which the medal is suspended. For every such Bar, a miniature insignia of a pattern approved by Government shall be added to the riband when worn alone.

701. **Mention in Desaptches:** A person is mentioned in despatches in recognition of meritorious services in operational areas and acts

of gallantry which are not of a sufficiently high order to warrant the grant of gallantry awards. A lotus leaf emblem is awarded to a person mentioned in desaptches. Posthumous awards can be made. All Army personnel including personnel of the Reserve Forces, personnel of the Territorial Army, Militia and other lawfully constituted Armed Forces, members of the Nursing Services and civilians working under or with the Armed Forces are eligible. There is no objection to a person's name being mentioned in more than one despatch. But he will not be issued with a second emblem.

702. Effective Date of Gallantry Awards: The effective date of an award will be determined as follows: –

(a) Where the specific operation in which the act of gallantry is performed extends to a single day or two days, the effective date would be that single day or the first of the two days.

(b) Where the citation quotes several acts occurring on separate dates at intervals, the effective date should be taken as the last day of the series of acts i.e., the final act which caused the recommendation to be submitted.

(c) Awards to PsW:

(i) When the act or acts relate to a period prior to capture, the principles in (a) and (b) above, whichever is appropriate, should be applied.

(ii) When the award has been made for an escape the effective date should be the date of joining the nearest military unit.

(d) Doubtful cases. Such cases. will be decided by the Military Secretary, Army Headquarters to whom the matter will be referred.

703. The Meritorious Service Medal and the Long Service and Good Conduct Medal: the following categories of personnel will be eligible for the awards:

(a) Meritorious Service Medal. The Meritorious Service Medal with annuity is awarded to a substantive Daffadar/ Havildar of the Army provided he has rendered fifteen (15) years service as combatant or non-combatant which

(i) counts for pension or gratuity;

(ii) is free from conviction by a court-martial;

(iii) has not more than five red ink entries in his conduct sheet and no red ink entry within five years preceding the date of recommendation.

(b) Long Service and Good Conduct Medal. The Long Service and Good Conduct Medal (with gratuity) is awarded to NCOs below the rank of Daffadar/Havildar namely, sowars, drivers and sepoys and non-combatants (enrolled) provided they have fifteen years combatant or non-combatant service which

(i) counts for pension or gratuity;

(ii) Is free from conviction by court-martial;

(iii) has not more than five red ink entries in the conduct sheet and no red ink entry within three years preceding the date of recommendation.

NOTE

A nalk or lance Daffadar who has been tried by a court-martial and reduced to the ranks for an offence which would not necessarily have involved trial as a sepoy, may be recommended for the medal if his conduct sheet shows five years continuous good service since reduction.

Individuals who distinguish themselves in the field after committing an offence which has rendered them ineligible for the award of the medals, may be recommended for the awards if, otherwise qualified, at the discretion of the OC.

704. Conditions Governing The Awards: These Awards are made twice a year, i.e., on 26th Jan and 15th Aug every year; the number of awards to be made on each occasion is determined as under :—

(a) Meritorious Service Medal. Awards of Meritorious Service Medal will be made against clear vacancies which occur upto the date preceding the date of the award. For example, awards against vacancies which occur during the period 26th Jan to 14th Aug are made from 15th Aug. Similarly awards against vacancies which occur during the period 15th Aug to 25th Jan will be made from 26th Jan.

NOTE

Vacancies for the Meritorious Service Medal occur on the death discharge, reduction, promotion to the commissioned rank or the forfeiture of the medal of an annuitant. Awards are only made against clear vacancies thus created in the allotted fixed quota for each regiment/corps.

(b) Long Service and Good Conduct Medal. 50 percent of the sanctioned number of awards is awarded from 26th Jan and the balance of 50 percent is awarded from 15th Aug of the year for which the awards are made, subject to the prescribed ceiling limit.

705. Scale of Medals: The scale of medals is as under:

(a) Meritorious Service Medal. 4 for 800 men on the authorized establishment of the Army.

(b) Long Service and Good Conduct Medal. 4 for 800 men on the authorized establishment of the Army.

706. Procedure for Submission of Recommendations for Meritorious Service Medal The Long Service and Good Conduct Medal:
(a) Officer Commanding units will recommend to the Officer-in-Charge Records concerned, the names of the individuals serving under them who are recommended for these medals. The following information will be furnished by the Officer Commanding.

(i) Regimental Number.

(ii) Rank.

(iii) Name.

(iv) Brief reasons in support of the recommendation.

(v) Character*

*As assessed by the Officer commanding in terms of Para 170(2) of the Regulations for the Army.

(b) On receipt of the information mentioned at (a) above, Officer-in-Charge Records will complete the form IAFY-1931 (Revised) in respect of each individual recommended for these awards and forward the same to the Commandant of the regimental or corps centre concerned.

(c) The Commandant of the regimental or corps centre will endorse his recommendations on the form and forward the same by 1st Jun/1st Nov preceding the date on which the awards are to be made to Army HQ (as shown below) together with his recommendation in regard to the order of preference in which the award should be made. Persons with 'exemplary' character only will be recommended.

(i) For Armoured Corps and Infantry to Adjutant General's Branch (AG/ CW-2), Army HQ

(ii) For all other arms or corps to the respective arms or corps director at Army Headquarters.

(d) The arms or corps directors concerned will scrutinize the recommendations and forward the following details to AG's Branch

(AG/CW-2) by 1st Jun/1st Dec preceding the date on which the awards are to be made:

(i) List of personnel selected for these awards.

(ii) List of personnel recommended as reserve in the order of preference. At least 50 per cent name should be included in the list.

707. Foreign and Commonwealth Awards: (a) Titles. No member of the Army will accept any title or any honour to which a title is attached from a Commonwealth or foreign country.

(b) Honours and Decorations which do not amount to titles. In all cases of such awards prior permission of the Government of India for the acceptance is required. The Government would not normally grant permission for such awards, except in rare cases. Even in these exceptional cases where acceptance of Decorations from other Governments has been permitted, the recipients may wear the decoration and the ribbon only during the visit of the Head of the State, the Prime Minister or other important dignitary of the country which awarded the decoration, e.g., at ceremonial and other functions arranged in honour of that dignitary or by decorees who may be attached to the Liaison Staff of the dignitary. Applications seeking permission for the acceptance of foreign awards will be submitted to Army HQ, AG's Branch through normal staff channels.

708. Forfeiture: (a) The various awards are liable to be forfeited in the following circumstances:

(i) Gallantry decorations. Any person who has been convicted of an offence for treason, sedition, mutiny, cowardice, desertion during hostilities, murder, dacoity, rape or any unnatural offence or administratively dismissed from service on similar grounds shall be liable at the discretion of the President to forfeit all the gallantry decorations which may have been awarded to him together with any pension/allowance appertaining thereto, not already paid. Every such case will be submitted to the Ministry of Defence by the Army HQ, MS Branch for obtaining the orders of the President. The cancellation and annulment of the awards would be notified in the Gazette of India, Forfeiture of awards will also entail surrender of the decorations.

(ii) Campaign and Commemorative medals/clasps. Any person who has been convicted of any of the offences specified in sub para (a) (i) above or desertion, or who is convicted by a criminal court or who is cashiered, dismissed or removed from the service, shall be liable at the discretion of the Government of India to forfeit any campaign medals.

The Government of India may withhold the grant of a war medal to any person who, in its opinion has not rendered approved service during the campaign for which the medal is granted. Any person who has deserted or who suffers death by sentence of a court-martial or who is cashiered, dismissed or removed from the service for misconduct occurring during an operation for which the medal is granted, may be deemed not to have rendered approved service.

(iii) Meritorious Service Medal and Long Service and Good Conduct Medal. Any person who suffers death by sentence of a court-martial, or is cashiered, dismissed or removed from the service for misconduct or who is convicted by a criminal court to a term of sentence for three years or more, shall forfeit any medal awarded for meritorious service (except for gallantry) or for long service and good conduct, or to which he may be entitled, together with any annuity or gratuity appertaining thereto not already paid.

(b) All individual cases with recommendations for forfeiture or otherwise of the medals and decorations, together with relevant documents, will be forwarded through normal staff channels, within three months of the event necessitating the forfeiture, to the Adjutant General's Branch, Army Headquarters, who will submit them to the Ministry of Defence.

709. Restoration: The various awards forfeited in accordance with para 708 shall be restored at the discretion of the competent authority in the following circumstances:

(a) Gallantry Awards. The awards may be restored at the discretion of the President. Upon the restoration having been approved by the President, it will be notified in the Gazette of India. Any allowance/ pension attached with the awards restored shall also be consequently restored as from the date of restoration.

(b) Campaign and commemorative medals/clasps. (i)Where a minimum of three years service (including approved service involving periodic training) has been rendered subsequent to release from imprisonment (or if not applicable, subsequent to the date of conviction) provided that no offence has been committed during such service as would normally disqualify the individual from the award of an "exemplary" character on discharge or transfer to the reserve.

In cases of desertion during a state of hostilities no awards instituted for service during the period of hostilities in which desertion took place will be restored unless the individual subsequently rendered approved service in the Armed Forces from which he deserted before the termination of the particular period of hostilities for which the award was instituted. In this respect approved service is deemed to be paid service of one day or more after release from imprisonment and before termination of the appropriate period of hostilities.

(ii) Where the required three years' requalifying service has not been completed owing to death, discharge, or release, wounds or sickness not due to misconduct, provided that no offence has been committed during the period between release from imprisonment (or, if not applicable subsequent to the date of conviction) upto the date of termination of service, as would normally disqualify the individual from the award of an "exemplary" character on discharge or transfer to the Reserve.

(iii) When the individual is permitted to re-engage for pension, after completion of the first period of service; or mobilized from the Reserve; or promoted to Havildar or higher rank.

(iv) At the discretion of the Government of India in recognition of meritorious service not necessarily resulting in decoration or when otherwise specially recommended.

(c) Meritorious Service Medal and/or Long Service and Good Conduct Medal. These awards together with any annuity or gratuit which may be payable, shall be restored at the discretion of t. Government of India.

All individual cases tor restoration of the medals and decorations standing forfeited and cancelled, together with relevant documents will be submitted to the Adjutant General's Branch, Army Headquarters, through normal staff channels, for obtaining the orders of the competent authority through the Ministry of Defence.

710. Disposal of Forfeited, Unclaimed and Undistributed Medals: Forfeited, unclaimed and undistributed medals will be returned to the Medal Section, Ministry of Defence, after the following time limits:

Gold and Silver Medals	two months
Other medals	one year
Campaign Stan, Medals and Commemorative Medals	Six years

711. Replacement of Medals: (a) Medals or decorations accidentally lost may be replaced on payment. The sanction of the Ministry of Defence will be necessary when it is proposed to replace them at the expense of the State. If in the opinion of the competent authority a medal has been made away with willfully or lost through carelessness, the man will be dealt with under Army Act (Act XLVI of 1950) Section 54.

(b) If a soldier is required to replace a medal willfully made away with or lost through carelessness he will be subjected to stoppages of the amount required to be paid for the duplicate, inclusive of authorized departmental expenses.

(c) Free replacement of medals and decoration will be made if it is established that the awardee has not received initial issue of the medal/ decoration and it is not in the possession of a Record Office or other forwarding agency. In all such cases the awardee must furnish a statutory declaration in the following form duly attested by the OC unit in the case of serving personnel and a magistrate in the case of non-effective personnel.

"STATUTORY DECLARATION FOR NON-RECEIPT OF MEDALS/ DECORATIONS TO WHICH CLAIMANT IS ENTITLED.

I, (No.)............ (Rank).......................... (Name)............... (Regiment)..................................... do hereby solemnly affirm that I have NOT yet received from any source the following medal(s) to which I am entitled for having served...(give details of operations during which service was rendered).

Name of medal(s)/decoration(s). ....(Signature of soldier)

Declared before me this................................ day of........................
Nineteen hundred and.......................... at...............................

(Signature of OC unit/magistrate whichever is applicable)

Designation................

(d) In all other cases duplicates will be issued on payment only. If an awardee does not pay the cost of replacement he will be issued with a certificate of entitlement and not the actual medal/ decoration.

(e) In the case of old British awards, duplicates will only be issued if available.

(f) Units/Record offices will ensure that medals/decorations when received from the Medal Section, Ministry of Defence, are delivered to awardees within the time limits shown below :

(i) Costly medals/decorations (Gold and silver)	Two months.
(ii) Campaign stars/medals and Commemorative medals	Six years
(iii) Other medals	One year.

Record offices will return the undistributed/unclaimed medals to the Medal Section, Ministry of Defence only after the expiry of the above time limit.

(g) Where a medal is lost from unit/record office prior to despatch to the decoree and responsibility for the loss cannot be placed on a particular individual, the cost of replacement is to be met by the units/centres from non-public funds.

(h) Application for replacement of medals on payment will be submitted on AFB-177 to the Medal Section, Ministry of Defence by the OC unit or head of the department concerned in the case of serving personnel. Before applying, the cost of the medal to be replaced will be ascertained from the Medal Section,

Ministry of Defence and the sum deposited in the nearest civil treasury or any branch of the State Bank of India for credit to the Controller of Defence Accounts, Central Command, Meerut. The receipted triplicate treasury receipt will be forwarded to the Medal Section, Ministry of Defence, with the application for replacement and the Medal Section will, after verification of the claim, send the treasury receipt with a forwarding memorandum to the Controller of Defence Accounts, Central Command Meerut for adjustment in his accounts. Care will be taken that the number, rank and spelling of the name in the application are exactly the same as on the original medal roll. Such medals of the non-effective personnel, when received from the Medal Section, will be disposed of in accordance with para 689.

(j) A commanding officer or other officer concerned will not countenance any attempt to replace lost war medals, except under the procedure outlined in this para.

712.Re-Issue of Medals/Decorations: Requests for the re-issue of medals which have already been returned to the Medal Section, Ministry of Defence, being undistributed/unclaimed, will be made once a month only, i.e., during the last week of each month, on the prescribed form. Piecemeal requests will not be entertained by the Medal Section.

713. Recording of The Grant, Forfeiture and Restoration of Medals - The grant, forfeiture and restoration of medals will be recorded in the Records Of Service in the case of officers and in Sheet Rolls in case of JCOs, WOs, OR and NCs(E). When medals are issued to a man after he has left the colours, the Officers i/c Records will enter the grant in the man's discharge or transfer documents.

714. Use of abbreviations for gallantry and other awards: — Recipients of gallantry decorations and other awards may use the following abbreviations after their names: —

PVC	—	For Param Vir Chakra
MVC	—	For Maha Vir Chakra
VrC	—	For Vir Chakra
AC	—	For Ashoka Chakra
KC	—	For Kirti Chakra
SC	—	For Shaurya Chakra
SYSM	—	For Sarvottam Yudh Seva Medal
UYSM	—	For Uttam Yudh Seva Medal
YSM	—	For Yudh Seva Medal
PVSM	—	For Param Vishisht Seva Medal
AVSM	—	For Ati Vishisht Seva Medal
VSM	—	For Vishisht Seva Medal
SM	—	For Sena Medal
NM	—	For Nao Sena Medal
VM	—	For Vayu Sena Medal

(b) The Symbol (a black square) denoting the award of BAR to a decoration referred to above, where applicable, may also be shown against the names of recipients in the Army List only.

(c) Abbreviations of pre-Independence gallantry awards, e.g., VC, MC and others conferred upon armed forces personnel will continue to be used after the names of the recipients. The procedure for denoting the award of Bar to a post-independence decoration in the Army list will also be applicable to Independence gallantry awards.

(d) No abbreviations will be used for any other awards.

715. Engraving of Medals: All medals will be duly engraved before issue by the Government of India.

716. Record of Receipt and Disposal of Medals/ Decorations: Receipts for medals/stars and decorations will be retained with individual's sheet rolls till these are destroyed as per the rules. Other papers connected with receipt and disposal of medals/stars decorations will be destroyed after a period of 6 years from the date of issue.

717. Order of Precedence of Awards: The order of precedence of various awards is as follows:

Bharat Ratna.

Param Vir Chakra

Ashoka Chakra.

Padma Vibhushan

Padma Bhusan

Param Vishisht Seva Medal

Maha Vir Chakra

Kirti Chakra.

Padma Shri.

Sarvottam Jeevan Raksha Padak.

Ati Vishisht Seva Medal

Vir Chakra.

Shaurya Chakra.

The President's Police and Fire Service Medal for gallantry

Sena/Nao Sena/Vayu Sena Medal

Vishisht Seva Medal

The Police Medal for gallantry.

Uttam Jeevan Raksha Padak.

Wound Medal.

The General Service Medal 1947

Samar Seva Star 1965

Poorvi Star.

Paschimi Star.

Raksha Medal 1965.

Sangram Medal.

Sainya Seva Medal

Police (Special Duty) Medal 1962

Videsh Seva Medal

The President's Police and Fire Service Medal for distinguished Service.

The Meritorious Service Medal

The Long Service and Good Conduct Medal

The Police Medal for meritorious service.

Jeevan Raksha Padak.

The Territorial Army Decoration

The Territorial Army Medal

The Indian Independence Medal 1947

The Independence Medal 1950

25th Independence Anniversary Medal

Vinsha Varsha Dirgha Seva Medal

Nava Varsha Dirgha Seva Medal

Commonwealth Awards

Other Awards

718. Supply of Medals/Decorations to Private Collectors, Institutions and Foreign Governments: (a) Private collectors and quasi-official institutions will not normally be supplied with specimens of medals and decorations except in very exceptional circumstances. In the exceptional cases in which it is decided to supply a specimen, this will ordinarily be on payment.

(b) Official institutions duly supported by a foreign government and foreign governments may be supplied specimens of medals, normally on payment, and in exceptional cases, especially where reciprocity is involved, gratis.

(c) All requests falling under sub paras (a) and (b) above will be referred to the Government of India for approval. Army

HQ and lower formations receiving such requests will forward them to the Medal Section, Ministry of Defence for further necessary action.

719. General Service Medal 1947: (a) this medal is awardable for service rendered with the Armed Forces under active service conditions or conditions akin thereto. Where appropriate, a clasp for each operation shall be instituted. An individual qualifying for the medal for the first time shall be awarded the medal together with a clasp indicating the particular operation for which it is awarded. For all subsequent operations for which the issue of a clasp is approved, the clasp indicating the particular operation shall only be awarded. The Bar of the clasp shall have the name or the place of the operation engraved on it.

(b) Persons eligible for the award are:

(i) Officers, men and women of all ranks of the Army, of any of the reserve forces, of the Territorial Army, Militia and of any other lawfully constituted Armed Forces;

(ii) Matrons, Sisters, Nurses and the staff of the Nursing Service and other Services pertaining to Hospital and Nursing;

(iii) Civilians on the authorized establishment of unit/formation of Armed Forces, who are enrolled or uniformed or liable for general service.

(c) The following clasps for this medal have so far been authorized:

(i) Clasp "Jammu and Kashmir – 1947". Authorized for service in Jammu and Kashmir operations between 27th Oct 47 and 1st Jan 49 for those who took part in battle or had put in an aggregate of 180 days service on the active strength of the unit/formation operating or located in specified operational or concessional areas.

(ii) Clasp "OVERSEAS KOREA 1950-53". Authorized for operational service rendered by Army personnel who served on the active strength of the 60th Para Field Ambulance unit in Korea between 22nd Nov 50 and 8th Jul 53.

(iii) Clasp "Naga Hills". Authorized for 180 days service on the active strength of a detachment/unit/formation in the following, singly or jointly, with effect from 27th Apr 55 :

(aa) OPG OLI from 27th Apr 55 to 1st Apr 56;

(ab) Operating or located under operational command of GOCAssam/23 INF Div/OP ORCHID/GOC NAGALAND/8 Mtn Div/GOC 101 Communication Zone Area.

(ac) For an aggregate of 90 days of service on the active strength of a detachment, unit or formation operating in Naga hills and Tuensang area on temporary duty with effect from 27th Apr 55 or thereafter.

(iv) Clasp "Goa – 1961". Authorized to Army personnel who were on the strength of or were attached to formations/units which participated in the operations and were within the geographical limits of the territories of Goa, Daman and Diu for not less than two days (48 hours) between 18th and 22nd Dec 61.

(v) Claps "Ladakh 1962 and NEFA 1962" – Authorized to Army personnel who rendered 15 days service with units/ formations within the geographical limits of Ladakh or certain specified areas of NEFA and Assam between 20th Oct 1962 and 21st Nov 62 and 21st Sep 62 and 2lst Nov 62 respectively.

(vi) Clasp "Mizo Hills". – Authorized to Army personnel who rendered an aggregate of 180 days service on the active strength of a detachment/unit/formation located or operated in Mizo Hills district with effect from 28th Feb 66, except those who have been temporarily inducted for specific operations. In the latter case the minimum qualifying service is 90 days.

720. Samar Seva Star: (a) Awarded to personnel who rendered at least ten days active service between 5th Aug 65 and 25th Jan 66 in a unit/formation operating or located in the qualifying areas specified for the purpose or personnel who served for a minimum qualifying period of one day in any battle zone, during the period specified for each battle zone.

(b) All officers, JCOs, OR, NCsE of Regular Army, Reserve, Territorial Army when embodied and militia forces and also civilians in their employment against authorized vacancies and "who formed part of these establishments are eligible for this award.

721. Raksha Medal 1965: This medal is awarded to all Armed Forces personnel who were born on the effective strength of the Armed Forces on 5 Aug 65 and had rendered service for 180 days or more on that date. The award may be made posthumously.

722. Navavarsha Dirgha Seva Medal and Vinsha Varsha Dirgha Seva Medal.- These medals are awardable to all categories of

Army personnel on completion of unblemished service of 9 and 20 years and more on 19th Apr 71 and thereafter.

723. Sangram Medal, Poorvi Star and Paschimi Star: The following medals are awarded to armed forces personnel and civilians in the Indo-Pak war 1971:

(a) Sangram Medal. This medal is awarded to all ranks of the Army, of any of the Reserve Forces, of the Territorial Army, J&K Militia and of any other armed forces of the Union who were on the effective strength of the armed forces on 3 Dec 71 or thereafter till the final disengagement and civilians of either sex serving regularly or temporarily under the orders/directions or supervision of the above mentioned forces in operational areas.

(b) Poorvi Star. :

(i) This medal is awarded to all ranks of the Army of any of the Reserve Forces, of the Territorial Army and J&K Militia and of any other armed forces of the Union who participated in operations in and around Bangladesh and civilians of either sex serving regularly or temporarily under the orders/ directions or supervision of the above forces. The minimum qualifying service is 1 day in the specified battle zones or 10 days in specified qualifying areas.

(ii) Period of eligibility: Battle Zones-3 Dec to 16 Dec 71 qualifying Areas – 25 Mar 71 to 25 Mar 72.

(c) Paschimi Star.

(i) This medal is awarded to all ranks of the Army, of any of the Reserve Forces, of the Territorial Army, J&K Militia and of any other armed forces of the Union who participated in operations against Pakistan forces in and around Western borders of India and civilians of either sex serving regularly or temporarily under the orders/ directions or supervision of the above forces. The minimum qualifying service is 1 day in the specified battle zones or 10 days in the specified qualifying areas.

(ii) Period of eligibility: The period of eligibility is from 3 Dec 71 to 20 Dec 72 (both days inclusive).

724. 25th Independence Anniversary Medal: This medal is awarded to all ranks of the Army, of any other Reserve Forces, Territorial Army, J&K Militia and any other armed forces of the Union who were borne on the effective strength of the armed forces on 15 Aug 72.

725. Wound Medal: This medal is awarded to all ranks of the Army, of any of the Reserve Forces, Territorial Army, J&K Militia and any other armed forces of the Union who sustained/sustain wounds as a result of direct enemy action in any type of operations or counter-insurgency operations with effect from 15 Aug 47. The award will not be made posthumously.

726. Samanya Seva Medal: (a) this medal is awardable for service rendered with the Armed Forces under active service conditions or conditions akin thereto on or after 26 Jan 65. Where appropriate, a clasp for each operation shall be instituted. An individual qualifying for the medal for the first time shall be awarded the medal together with a clasp indicating the particular operation for which it is awarded. For all subsequent operations for which the issue of a clasp is approved, the clasp indicating the particular operation shall only be awarded. The bar of the clasp shall have the name or the place of the operation engraved on it.

(b) The following categories of personnel serving in an operation or concessional area within the territorial or time limits to be specified separately for each operation will be eligible for the award :

(i) All ranks of the Army, and of the Reserve, Territorial and militia forces, and civilians of either sex in all walks of life.

(ii) All other lawfully constituted forces and security forces operating under the operational control of the Regular Armed Forces.

(c) The following clasps for this medal have been authorized: –

(i) Clasp 'Kutch-Kargil 1965'. - The clasp will be admissible to: –

(aa) Personnel who rendered at least ten days active service in a unit/formation operating or located in specified qualifying areas between 9 Apr 1965 and 1 Jul 1965 or 1 day service in specified battle zone between 9 Apr 1965 and 1 May 1965 in Kutch Sector.

(ab) Personnel who rendered at least 90 days active service in a unit/formation operating or located in specified qualifying areas between 17 May 1965 and 25 January 1966 or 1 day service in specified battle zones between 17 May 1965 and 25 January 1966 in KARGIL Sector

(ac) Air crew personnel and personnel of ejection crew of air dispatch units who flew 1 sortie or 3 hours of flying in Kutch sector or 3 sorties or 10 hours of flying in Kargil sector during the specified period (ad) Personnel who died in service or were evacuated as a result of wounds or other disabilities attributable to service in specified areas irrespective of time limit

(ae) Personnel who won a gallantry decoration or a Mention-in-Despatch es for service in specified areas irrespective of the time-limit

(ii) Clasp 'Nathula-Chola 1967':- The clasp will be admissible to:

(aa) Personnel who were actually deployed and took part in the border incidents at Nathula between 11 and 16 Sep 1967 or Chola on 1 Oct 1967 and rendered at least one day's service in that area.

(ab) Personnel who were wounded, killed or earned a gallantry award or Mention-in-Despatch es during the above mentioned incidents irrespective of time-limit.

(ac) Personnel who flew one sortie over the Nathula or Chola area in performance of duty.

(iii) Clasp 'Mizoram'. The clasp will be admissible to:

(aa) Personnel who have put in an aggregate of 180 days of service on the active strength of a detachment/unit/ formation located or operating in qualifying areas singly or jointly from 8 May 1975 or thereafter except those who have been temporarily inducted for specific operation; in the latter case the minimum qualifying service is 90 days.

(ab) Air crew personnel and personnel of Army Air Transport Organisation, Rear Air-field Supply Organisation, Air Despatch Units and Air Observation Post units, who carried out a minimum of five operational sorties of 20 hours of flying over the qualifying areas from 8 May 1975 or thereafter

(ac) Personnel who win a gallantry award or a Mention-in-Despatch es or die or sustain wounds or other disability while on service in the area irrespective of time-limit during the qualifying period.

The time spent in hostile captivity in consequence of capture during service in the area will count towards the qualifying period for the award of the clasp.

(ad) Naval personnel attached to the Army or the Air force, including those serving with Border Road Organisation in the qualifying area, shall be eligible for the award according to the conditions of eligibility applicable to the service to which they are attached.

Service in Mizoram will not count for the eligibility of Sainya Seva Medal with clasp 'Bengal-Assam' with effect from 8 May 1975. If, however, an individual falls short of the aggregate number of days required to qualify for 'Bengal-Assam clasp and also for 'Mizoram' clasp in the area and if his service is continuous, he may be permitted to count the period beyond 8 May 1975 to make up an aggregate number of days required for 'Bengal-Assam' clasp to the Sainya Seva Medal.

(iv) Clasp- 'Tlrap' – the clasp will be admissible to:

(aa) Personnel who have put in an aggregate of 180 days of service on the active strength of a detachment/ unit/ formation operating or located in Tirap District under operational command of 51 Mtn Artillery Brigade/192 Mountain Brigade under 2 Mtn Div w. e. f. 1 Jun 1979 or thereafter except those who have been temporarily inducted for specific operation; in the latter case the minimum qualifying service is 90 days.

(ab) Ejection crews of Ait Despatch units and personnel borne on the effective strength of Army Air Transport Organisation, Rear Airfield Supply Organisation, Air Despatch Units and Air Observation post Units and of Headquarters 2 Mtn Div and 51 Mtn Artillery Bde who carried out a minimum of five operational or reconnaissance sorties or 20 hours of flying in Tirap District with effect from 1 Jun 1979 or thereafter.

(ac) Personnel who died in service or were evacuated as a result of wounds or other disabilities attributable to service in field area in Tirap District irrespective of time limit or number of sorties or number of operational flying hours.

(ad) Personnel who won a decoration or Mention-in-Dispatches for service in Tirap District irrespective of time limit or number of sorties or number of operational flying hours, Time spent in hostile captivity in consequence of capture during service in Tirap District will count towards the qualifying period for the medal and the clasp.

SECTION FIVE

The Defence Simulation Glossary provides Defence with an endorsed simulation-specific glossary for consistent utilization in Defence.

The terminologies and abbreviations in the Glossary are as simulation-focused as practical with minimum overlap with other related glossary in Defence such as Information Technology & Communications Glossary, Architecture Glossary, Geospatial Glossary and other terms which are already featured in the Defence Glossary.

Executive Summary – The Defence Glossary

The rate of change of technologies and markets in the last several years has been greater than at any other time in history. This rapid change has brought with it a wealth of opportunities for those who know how to embrace it, and a whole new class of threats for those who don't. To survive in the new world, an organization must be nimble, resourceful, and confident. Or more accurately, its decision makers must exhibit those qualities. Many enterprises finding success in this climate of change are doing so by leveraging a proven learning technology called Business Simulation.

Early adopters of Business Simulation are using it primarily to enable strategic change. Business Simulation applications immerse the student in a simulated environment where he or she can practice tasks to master skill and gain understanding. It has been shown in study after study that the learner will achieve higher degrees of retention and cognition than by other methods of instruction. Business Simulations are commonly described as flight simulators for business.

Learning by Doing

The overarching theme in a business simulation is that the student learns by doing. The actual work environment is simulated and the student performs the tasks that they will have to perform on the job. In a flight simulator, the pilot takes off, flies a pattern, and lands. Along the way, unpredictable incidents may occur and the pilot must address and resolve them or risk crashing. In a business simulation, the student performs activities such as starting a company, creating a production strategy, and defending an investment plan to a board of directors. Unexpected events or changes in the business climate arise that the student is challenged to resolve.

Risk Free

Business simulations allow the student to learn how to navigate very treacherous situations without risk. In a flight simulator, a pilot can learn to recover from wind shear or land a plane with an engine fire by trying different techniques until he or she is very skilled at knowing what works and what doesn't. In a business simulation, a student can repeatedly attempt to recover from poor cash positions, labor disputes, manufacturing snafus, and the like, without risking the financial health of a real company. All the while the student is learning from successes and failures.

Time Compression

In real life it may take years to become very skilled in a particular field, largely because it may take years to encounter all of the business situations that may arise in the field. It also may take years for the results of strategic business decisions to unfold and it may be difficult to see how specific outcomes tie back to the original decisions. Business simulation compresses time-to-competency in two ways. It exposes the student to a broad array of scenarios in a short period of time, and the student can see the results of decisions play out in a few seconds, so it's easier to relate to outcomes.

Realistic Simulation

Flight simulators have varying degrees of fidelity. Some have cartoon-like graphics, some have photo-realistic graphics, some have very accurate representations of the cockpit and controls. Some even have walk-in cockpits that move and roll to give physical feedback. Similarly, business simulations have varying degrees of fidelity and sophistication. Some have relatively simple tasks, like balancing a checkbook, and the student is only told if the task has been completed correctly or incorrectly. Others have very complex tasks with a variety of solutions, none of which is completely correct. The student must evaluate subtle tradeoffs like how much money to invest in machinery to reduce labor costs, or whether to rely on contractors rather than hire full time employees.

Intelligent Integration

One feature of business simulations that helps make them effective is the use of simulated personalities that interact with the student. These agents may play the role of subordinates, peers, mentors, or adversaries. They can help guide the student to successfully navigate the simulation, or they may challenge the student to find innovative ways to succeed in the face of competition. For example, the student might get advice from several simulated team members in creating a business plan. The student might then defend the plan to a panel of simulated investors to get startup money.

Based on Sound Learning Theory

Business simulations wrap the content and the learner in an engaging story where the learner pursues business objectives. Humans have evolved to learn well from stories and cognitive research has borne this out. Also, content is not pushed at the learner at a moment when he or she might not be receptive to it. Instead the learner pulls content as needed to achieve the goal, thus increasing retention.

LEARNER PACED/ LEARNER DIRECTED/ LEARNER LOCATED/ LEARNER SCHEDULED

Because business simulations are computer-based, the student can go as slowly or as quickly as appropriate. The learner can repeat parts of the simulation as frequently as desired to hone skills. Business simulations can be delivered via the Web or even on CD-ROM to maximize location and scheduling convenience for the learner.

Expert Content and Advice

One of the most value-enhancing features of new business simulations is the pervasive integration of expert content and advice. Media-intense reference materials can introduce the learner to the content in a structured, intuitive fashion, leaving the learner able to explore at will. Video war stories from veteran experts can help the student get an insider's viewpoint into the business area being simulated. Artificially intelligent agents can watch every move and decision the student makes to provide customized, intelligent feedback that fosters understanding and motivates learning.

Comprehensive Learning Experience

When coupled with online reference materials and expert/peer discussion sessions, business simulation can act as the centerpiece of a comprehensive learning experience. Learning by doing in a risk-free, time-compressed environment with intelligent interaction and support is the fastest and most effective way to build confidence and competency in your workforce.

Terms and Definitions

Accreditation: The official certification that a model, simulation or federation of models and/or simulations is acceptable for use for a specified purpose.

Accreditation agent: The organisation designated by the application sponsor to conduct an accreditation assessment for a simulation application or element.

Accuracy: The degree of exactness of a model or simulation, high accuracy implying low error.

Agent: A computer system, program element or entity that to some extent is capable of autonomous action.

Note: this includes deciding for itself what is needed to satisfy design objectives, and being capable of interaction with other agents

Agent based modeling: A specified and logical model representation intended for replication and use in computer modeling and simulation.

Note: agent based modeling includes representative behaviours including cognitive and social representation, which manifests in the actions and characteristics of an agent. This in turn is influenced by the actions and characteristics of other real or modeled agents in a social system

Artifact: All the relevant capability elements, including equipment, software, hardware, and associated documents such as standards,

Standard Operating Procedures (SOPs), Tactics, Techniques and Procedures (TTPs) and policies, which are physically and temporarily brought together to produce a system.

Artificial intelligence 1(AI): The capacity or function of a device, system or agent to automate functions which are typically associated with human intelligence.

Artificial intelligence 2(AI): A branch of computer science associated with machine intelligence.

Asset management: The strategic process by which systems or facilities is monitored and maintained, with the objective of providing the best possible service to the user.

Augmented reality (AR): A type of virtual reality in which synthetic stimuli are registered with and superimposed on real world objects, often used to make information otherwise imperceptible to human senses, perceptible.

Note: the merging of real-world and virtual reality to produce new environments where physical and digital objects can co-exist and interact in real time, to include augmented reality

Augmented reality (wearable): With augmented reality, a participant wears a see-through display or views video of the real world with an opaque head mounted display that allows graphics or text to be projected in the real world

Augmented reality/mixed reality: A field of computer research which deals with the combination of real-world and computer-generated data.

Augmented virtuality (AV): The merging of real world objects into virtual worlds.

Australian Defence Simulation Office (ADSO): A directorate of Simulation Branch within the Vice Chief of the Defence Force Group, responsible for the delivery of simulation governance, enterprise simulation capability services and the coordination and collaboration of simulation activities across Defence.

Automated forces (AF): The most automated of the computer-generated forces, which require little or no human interaction.

Autonomous entity: A battle space entity that does not require the presence of another battle space entity to conduct its own simulation in the battle space environment.

Note: all Distributed Interactive Simulation (DIS) compliant battle space entities are autonomous in that they are responsible for creating their own view of the environment

Base Object Model (BOM): A single aspect of federation interplay, which can be used as a building block of Federation Object Models (FOMs) and Simulation Object Models (SOMs).

Battle space: Refers to both the physical environment in which the simulated warfare will take place, and the forces that will conduct the simulated warfare.

Battle space entity: A simulation entity that corresponds to actual equipment, supplies, and personnel, which typically is seen or sensed on a real operational environment.

Behavioural modeling: Modeling of representative entity behaviours in which individual or group behaviours are derived from the physical, psychological or social characteristics of the sentient and non-sentient systems represented

Belief-desire-intention (BDI) framework: A model of human reasoning processes, developed for programming intelligent agents.

Certification: The determination that a simulation process, data set, hardware, or vehicle meets a standard or predefined set of terms and conditions.

Closed-loop simulation: A simulator or simulation system with an active feedback loop.

Closed standard (deprecated): A file format, protocol, or program that does not comply with the requirements for a free or open standard.

Notes:

1.Examples include file formats or protocols whose specifications are not publicly available, software whose source code is not available and patent-encumbered technologies.

2.Closed standards are typically developed by private companies with limited public or industry participation

Preferred term: proprietary standard

Collaborative environment: Multiple users interacting within a simulation that enables interaction among participants, not necessarily manifested in virtual reality (VR).

Note: A collaborative VR environment can be referred to as multi-presence or multi-participant

Combat modeling: Any structural activity, varying in degrees of abstraction and reality, undertaken to represent combat and associated battle space functions and effects.

Common services, applications and data: Services, applications and data which are, or potentially can be, used (and reused) by more than one simulation system/user (client) and for which benefits can be realised by making them discoverable and available through the Defence Synthetic Environment (DSE).

Compliant: A simulation or simulator that is produced or manufactured in accordance with the prescribed standards.

Computer aided learning: A method of instruction which uses computer technology in collaboration with, or replacement of traditional text and classroom-based teaching.

Computer generated forces (CGF): A computer representation of forces in simulations which attempt to model human behaviour sufficiently so that forces will take some actions automatically, without requiring human-in-the-loop interaction.

Notes:

1.CGFs may be fully autonomous, needing no human direction, or semi-autonomous, requiring some direction by a human controller.

2.CGFs represent friendly, opposing, and neutral battle space participants not portrayed by manned simulators

Conceptual model: A statement of the content and internal representations that are the users and developers combined representation of the model.

Note: it includes logic and algorithms and explicitly recognizes assumptions and limitations

Confidence building approach: A simulation application execution which ensures that a simulation system adequately fits the simulation end-users' business and technical needs.

Note: the following three perspectives need to be considered: what informal approaches might be appropriate; what formal standards and processes might be appropriate; and how to approach any residual concerns that might remain in order to build confidence in proceeding with the proposal simulation project.

Constructive simulation: A simulation involving simulated control entities (including agents) operating simulated battle space systems.

Notes:

1. Real people make inputs to such simulations, but are not directly involved in determining the outcomes.

2. A constructive simulation is a computer program or software element.

a. User interaction is typically through a control station (keyboard, mouse or handheld controller), which is not representative of a real system. For example, a military user may input data instructing a unit to move or engage an enemy target.

b. The constructive simulation determines the speed of movement, the effect of the engagement with an enemy, and any battle damage that may occur.

Continuous simulation: A simulation that uses a continuous model.

Notes:

1. Implies that the state (dependent) variables change in a continuous manner over time.

2. Contrast with: discrete event simulation

Control station: A facility which provides the interfaces for the individual responsible for manipulating the simulation, and provides the capacity to implement simulation control.

Data: A representation of facts, concepts, or instructions presented in a formalized manner suitable for communication, interpretation or processing by humans or automatic means.

Data certification: The determination that data meets a standard or predefined set of terms and conditions with respect to its intended use.

Data lag: The physical demonstration of data latency.

Data latency: The time interval required for a device to begin the output of data after presented with a stimulus or stimuli (i.e. input of data, occurrence of an event)

Data logger: A device which accepts data outputs from a simulation or federation, and stores them for later replay in the same time sequence as the data was originally received.

Data validation: The documented assessment of simulation data by subject area experts and its comparison to known values, in the context of its intended use.

Data verification: The use of techniques and procedures to ensure data meets constraints defined by data standards and business rules, derived from process and data modeling.

Data verification, validation and certification: The process of verifying the internal consistency, validating that it represents real world entities appropriate for its intended purpose or range of purposes, and certifying it has having a specified level of quality, appropriate for a specified use, type of use, or range of uses.

De facto standard: Standards those are commonly used, but are not official.

Dead reckoning: The process of extrapolating the position/orientation of an entity, based upon the last known position/orientation, velocity, and (sometimes) higher-order derivatives of position versus time and/or other vehicle dynamic characteristics.

Note: typically used in distributed simulation to compensate for data lag.

Defence Simulation Architecture (DSA): Describes the Defence Simulation Capability (DSC).

Notes:

1.The DSA is a compliant segment of the Defence Enterprise Architecture.

a. It provides an overall structure and scope of the DSC, as well as detailing views of the specific technical descriptions and integration protocols required for the governance of the DSC, including its development.

b. In capability development terms, the DSA is progressively acquired by the full suite of acquisition methods, including non-equipment procurement (NEP), rapid acquisition (RA), minor and major capital projects, including projects where simulation is part of a larger capability.

Defence Simulation Capability (DSC): Simulation in Defence is a Joint Enabling Capability.

Notes:

1. Referred to as The Defence Simulation Capability (DSC), it is a governed matrix of computer-based constructive and virtual envi-

ronments, which includes data exchange with instrumented live ranges and systems, distributed and stand alone systems.

2. In general, it includes simulations owned and used by Defence and those used and owned on behalf of Defence. The strategic purpose of simulation in Defence is articulated in the Simulation Strategy and Roadmap.

Defence Simulation Policy: The set of guidelines and principles used to achieve practical and effective outcomes of the Defence investment in and use of simulation as an enterprise enabling capability.

Notes:

1.The policy does not constrain the procedural application of simulation in single service domains or independent commands but is designed to provide a framework of principles to ensure that independent investments in simulation can be of benefit to the broader enterprise community.

2.Simulation policy is contained in Defence Instructions co-signed by the Secretary for Defence and the Chief of the Defence Force which provide a binding endorsement across all groups and financial entities of Defence.

Defence Simulation Vision: Simulation is an integrated enterprise capability that enables Defence to:

1. Lift the excellence of individual and collective training;

2. Analyze and fully understand the cost of ownership and capability; and

3. Provide enhanced support to decision makers in a cost effective and efficient manner

Defence Synthetic Environment (DSE): The DSE is a time and task-based configuration managed environment, comprising 'common' services, data and applications, hosted on public, Defence and specialized networks. The DSE is constructed as a Service Oriented Architecture environment to facilitate evolution and component reuse as Defence's demand for simulation evolves. The DSE is compatible with Defence's preferred ICT architecture.

Degrees of freedom (DOF): Refers to the number of simultaneous directions or inputs a sensor can measure or a simulator system can replicate.

Note: typically used to describe the combination of spatial positions and orientation.

Deterministic simulation: A simulation which, for a given set of inputs, produces an identical set of outputs, each time the simulation is run.

Note: the effect of changing a variable can be clearly determined.

Discrete event simulation: A simulation that uses a discrete model where the dependent variables (i.e. state indicators) change discretely at points in time referred to as events.

Note: contrast with: continuous simulation.

Distributed Interactive Simulation (DIS) Is an IEEE standard (1278) for conducting real-time war gaming across one or more host Computers.

Notes:

1.A synthetic environment is created through real-time exchange of IEEE 1278 compliant protocol data units between distributed, computationally autonomous simulation applications in the form of simulations, and instrumented equipment interconnected through standard computer communicative services.

2.The computational simulation entities may be present in one location or may be distributed geographically.

Domain: The physical or abstract simulation space in which the entities and processes operate.

Note: the domain can be land, sea, air, space, undersea, a combination of any of the above, or an abstract domain, such as an n-dimensional mathematics space, economic or psychological domains

Embedded simulation: A simulation that is built into, or added into, operational systems to enhance capability.

Note: Modern battle space systems typically include embedded simulation to aid training outcomes.

Emulation: A functionally exact representation of a system or component which may operate in real time or at a modified speed.

Note: this may exist as a physically exact replica of an operational item in an immersive simulation environment.

Emulator: - A device, computer program, or system that performs emulation.

Entity: Any component in a system that requires explicit representation in a model.

Note: Entities possess attributes denoting specific properties.

Examples: platform (ship, submarine, aircraft), munitions (missile, torpedo), a human being, or any other component that interacts with the simulation.

Environment: The texture or detail of the natural domain that is terrain relief, weather, day/night, terrain cultural features; and the external objects, conditions, and processes that influence the behaviour of a system.

Environmental Entity: A simulation entity that corresponds to dynamic elements of the natural state of the geographic, atmospheric and bathysphere environment, of the synthetic environment, that can be seen or sensed on a real battlefield.

Examples: craters, smoke, building collapse, weather conditions, and sea state.

Environmental representation: A representation of all or part of the natural or man-made environment, including permanent or semi-permanent man-made features

Event: A change of object attributes value, an interaction between objects, and an instantiation of a new object, or a deletion of an existing object that is associated with a particular point on the simulation time axis

Exercise: A military manoeuvre or simulated warfare operation involving planning, preparation, and execution.

Notes: 1.It is carried out for the purpose of training and evaluation.

EJB - Enterprise Java Bean

Emulation is imitation of a system where the imitation provides the exact desired functionality of the system.

The difference between simulation and emulation is that simulation uses a model, which is abstract and an approximation, but the emulation uses a representation intended to provide the exact functionality of the system emulated.

Encapsulation: In the Object-Oriented Paradigm: Encapsulation means that a consumer sees only the services that are available from an object, but not how those services are implemented.

Endogenous Activity is produced within the system resulting from internal causes.

Entity denotes an element of interest in the system.

Event is a change in the state of an object at a particular instant of time.

Exogenous Activity is produced within the system environment and affects the system. **Exogenous** activities are inputs to a system.

Feasibility of a requirement is the degree of difficulty of implementing a single requirement, and simultaneously meeting competing requirements. Sometimes requirements conflict with each other. It may be possible to achieve a requirement by itself, but it may not be possible to achieve a number of them simultaneously.

Financial Independence implies that the IV&V / Certification Agent is allocated its own budget for the M&S application V&V / Certification and does not rely on the M&S application development budget.

Formal VV&T Techniques are based on mathematical proof of correctness. If attainable, proof of correctness is the most effective means of M/S V&V.

Functional requirements Statements of services the model should provide, how the model should react to particular inputs and how the model should behave in particular situations. Functional requirements are requirements about the input-output transformations of the simulation model.

Functionality is the degree to which the M&S application completely captures all of the desired functional modules that need to be present.

Gaming-based M&S is the one which uses humans as part of its model. It is typically intended to train people. For example: Management Games are performed to train managers for a business. War Gaming is performed to train military commanders. The gaming known as Video Games are simulations that are intended for entertainment, educational or training purposes. Gaming-based M&S is typically used in disciplines such as Business, Education, Management, and Training.

Garbage-in garbage-out refers to a simulation with insufficient credibility.

Hardware-in-the-loop M&S can be viewed as Simulation-based Hardware Evaluation. A hardware system can be operated under simulated input conditions for the purpose of evaluating how well the hardware functions under such input conditions. For example, a space vehicle can be operated under simulated input conditions for the purpose of evaluating the vehicle's autopilot mode. Hardware-in-the-loop M&S is a cost-effective method for evaluating a complex, mission-critical hardware before it is used in the real world.

High Level Architecture (HLA) is a general purpose architecture that facilitates interoperability among network-centric simulations and enables reuse of simulations and their components. HLA-compliant simulations running on different hardware platforms can interoperate with each other over a network. Interoperability among the network-centric simulations is enabled by a RunTime Infrastructure (RTI).

HLA is an IEEE Standard, a DoD Standard, and a NATO Standard.

HTML- HyperText Markup Language

HTTP- HyperText Transfer Protocol

Human-in-the-loop M&S is also called Simulation-based Training. A simulation model of a system, e.g., airplane, air traffic control center, emergency management plan, or military operation is developed for the purpose of training people. Trainees interact with the visual simulation model for the purpose of learning, e.g., how to fly an airplane (using the flight simulator), how to control air traffic at an airport, how to manage an emergency in response to a disaster, or how to make military decisions. Human-in-the-loop M&S can also be used as a cost-effective method for evaluating human performance and behavior for a proposed system design.

IDE - Integrated Development Environment

IDL - Interface Definition Language

Implementation is the process of programming a simulation model design specification in a simulation software product or a high-level programming language such as Java or C++.

Inheritance In the Object-Oriented Paradigm: When an object is declared as member of a class, it inherits the characteristics (instance variables) and behaviors (instance methods) of that class as well as the characteristics and behaviors of that class's superclass, and any ancestral classes, tracing back to the root class. Inheritance significantly facilitates reusability of earlier developed classes and decreases simulation model development time.

Informal VV&T Techniques are called informal because the tools and approaches used rely heavily on human reasoning and subjectivity without stringent mathematical formalism. The "informal" label does not imply any lack of structure or formal guidelines for the use of the techniques. In fact, these techniques are applied using well structured approaches under formal guidelines and they can be very effective especially during the early stages of the M&S life cycle.

Instantiation In the Object-Oriented Paradigm: Creation of an object belonging to a class is called instantiation. The new object inherits all characteristics (instance variables) and behaviors (instance methods) specified in the class from which it is instantiated. Instance variables of a class are created for each object instantiated as a member of that class. Instance methods are inherited, but no method code is replicated.

Intended Use refers to the explicitly and clearly defined purpose for which the simulation model is intended for use.

IV&V Independent - Verification and Validation

Java EE - Java Platform, Enterprise Edition (Java EE)

JSF - Java Server Face

JSP - Java Server Page

Junk-input junk-output- Refers to a simulation with insufficient credibility.

Life Cycle - The M&S Life Cycle represents a framework for organization of the processes, work products, quality assurance activities, and project management activities required to develop, use, maintain, and reuse an M&S application from birth to retirement, and is created to modularize and structure an M&S application development and to provide guidance to an M&S developer (engineer), manager, organization, and community of interest.

Linear Mode is the one which describes relationships in linear form. The equation $y = 3x + 4z + 1$ is a linear model.

M&S - Modeling and Simulation

M/S - Model and/or Simulation

Ms/Ss - Models and/or Simulations

Managerial Independence - implies that the IV&V / Certification Agent reports to the M&S application sponsor independently of the M&S application developer organization.

Methods (Services) - In the Object-Oriented Paradigm: Services provided and behaviors exhibited by an object are specified in methods. Two types of methods exist: class methods and instance methods.

Class Methods - are used to provide services specific to a class. For example, the method "new" which creates an instance of a class.

Instance Methods, given in a class, are used to specify the services provided and behavior exhibited for each object instantiated from that class. Each instance (i.e., instantiated object) created as belonging to a class provides the services and behavior specified in the instance methods of that class. The method code is specified only once in the class and is not replicated for each instantiation of an object from that class.

Model is a representation and abstraction of anything such as a real system, a proposed system, a futuristic system design, an entity, a phenomenon, or an idea.

Model Builder's Risk is the probability of committing the Type I Error.

Model Instrumentation refers to the insertion of additional code (probes, stubs or trap code) into the executable model or sub model (module) for the purpose of collecting information about model behavior during execution. Probe locations are determined manually or automatically based on static analysis of model structure.

Model User's Risk - is the probability of committing the Type II Error.

Modeling is the act of constructing a model. Modeling is an artful balancing of opposites; on the one hand, a model should not contain unnecessary details and become needlessly complex and difficult to analyze, on the other hand, it should not exclude the essential details of what it represents.

Modifiability of a requirement - is the degree to which the requirement can easily be changed.

Monte Carlo M&S - is the one which uses a model built based on statistical random sampling. The model typically does not represent time-varying relationships. Monte Carlo M&S is typically used in disciplines such as Chemistry, Computational Engineering, Financial Probabilistic Modeling, Mathematics, Nuclear Engineering, (Computational, Nuclear, Statistical) Physics, and Reliability Engineering.

Network-Centric Simulation Architecture refers to the fundamental organization of simulation components that interoperate over a network, relationships among the simulation components, and the principles and guidelines governing the design and evolution of those simulation components.

We use the term "network" to refer to one or a combination of many types of communications networks such as Global System for Mobile communication (GSM), Internet, local area network (LAN), mobile ad-hoc network (MANET), virtual private network (VPN), or wireless network.

Nominal Score - is a named score such as excellent, good, fair, or poor.

Nonadaptive System - is a system which does not react to changes in its environment.

Non-functional requirements - Are requirements that are unrelated to functionality of the simulation model such as requirements for interoperability, performance, usability, standards, delivery, and portability.

Nonlinear Model - is the one which describes relationships in nonlinear form. The equation $F = (2x + 4z - 2) / (3y - x)$ is a nonlinear model.

Numerical Model - is the one which is solved by applying computational procedures. Finding the roots of a nonlinear algebraic equation, $f(x) = 0$, using the method of Interval Halving or Simple Iteration involves the use of a numerical model. System Simulation is considered to be a numerical computation technique.

Object denotes an element of interest in the system.

In the Object-Oriented Paradigm: An object is an entity which has a state and a defined set of operations which operate on that state. The state is represented as a set of object attributes. The operations associated with the object provide services to other objects which request these services when needed. Objects are created according to some object class definition. An object class definition serves as a template for objects. It includes declarations of all the attributes and services which should be associated with an object of that class.

Open System - is a system which has exogenous activities.

ORB - Object Request Broker

Parallel M&S is the one which executes its model parts (e.g., submodels, model components, subcomputations) on different processors of the same computer for the purpose of achieving faster execution time.

Passive Stakeholder is the one who will not actively interact with the system or product (e.g., M&S application) once it is operational and in use. Examples: M&S application developers, decision makers about the use of the M&S application, logistics personnel, manufacturer, owners/sponsors if they don't use/operate the M&S application.

Performance is the degree to which the M&S application executes its work in a speedy, efficient, and productive manner.

Physical Model is the one which is usually a physical replica, often on a reduced scale, of the system it represents. A physical model "looks like" the object it represents and is also called an Iconic Model. A model of an airplane (scaled down), a model of the atom (scaled up), a map, a globe, a model car are examples of physical (iconic) models.

Polymorphism in the Object-Oriented Paradigm: Polymorphism refers to the ability of an object to assume more than one form.

Prescriptive or Normative Model is a model which describes the behavior of a system with a value judgment on the "goodness" or "badness" of such behavior. A Linear Programming model, a Mixed Integer Linear Programming model and a nonlinear optimization model are examples of prescriptive models. When solved, these models provide a description of the solution as optimal, suboptimal, feasible, infeasible, etc.

Presentation is the process of interpretation of the simulation results, documentation of the simulation results, and communication of the simulation results to the decision makers.

Problem Formulation is the process by which the initially communicated problem is transformed into a formulated problem sufficiently well defined to enable specific research action.

Process is the succession of states of an object over a span which is the contiguous succession of one or more intervals.

Pseudo-Random Number Generation: Refers to the generation of random numbers in a way that is reproducible by using a starting value called seed. Pseudo implies that the numbers are not truly random, but satisfy statistical properties for randomness.

Quality Assurance (QA) of M/S refers to the planned and systematic activities that are established throughout the M&S life cycle to substantiate adequate confidence that a M/S possesses a set of characteristics needed and expected by the user for a set of intended uses.

Random Variable is a real-valued function that maps a sample space into the real line (numbers). Example random variable: Interarrival Time (X)

Random Variate is a particular outcome or sample value of a random variable. Example: 26 as a particular value of the random variable X.

RDBMS - Relational Data Base Management System

Requirements Engineering is the process of elicitation of requirements based on the formulated problem, and specification of the requirements in an authoritative manner. This process takes the formulated problem as input and produces a M&S requirements specification document (RSD) as the output work product.

RMI - Remote Method Invocation

RSD - Requirements Specification Document

RVG - Random Variate Generation

Self-Driven Simulation is the one which uses random numbers in sampling from probability distributions so as to drive the model.

Simulation - To Simulate, according to Webster's Dictionary, is:"To feign, to attain the essence of without the reality" To Simulate, in simple terms, implies to imitate or mimic.

Simulation is the act of executing, experimenting with or exercising a model for a specific objective such as acquisition, analysis (problem solving), education, entertainment, research, or training.

SOA - Service-Oriented Architecture

SOAP - Simple Object Access Protocol, an XML-based messaging protocol used to encode the information in web service request and response messages before sending them over a network.

Software-in-the-loop M&S can be viewed as Simulation-based Software Evaluation. A software system can be executed under simulated input conditions for the purpose of evaluating how well the software system functions under such input conditions. For example, the software used to display the common operating picture (COP) in a combat operation on a handheld computer can be executed under simulated input data (e.g., video, voice, images, text) received from many different sources for the purpose of evaluating how well the software satisfies its requirements. Software-in-the-loop M&S is a cost-effective method for evaluating a complex, mission-critical software system before it is used in the real world.

SQL - Structured Query Language

Stability of requirements is the degree to which the requirements are changing while the M&S application is under development.

Stable Model is the one which tends to return to its initial condition after being disturbed. Like a simple pendulum that is set in motion, it may overshoot and oscillate, but the disturbances decline and die out.

State of an object is the enumeration of all attribute values of that object at a particular instant of time.

State of a system is the exhaustive enumeration of all attribute values (of all objects) at a particular instant of time.

Static Model is the one which describes relationships that do not change with respect to time. An architectural model of a house which helps us visualize floor plans and space relationships is a static physical model. An equation relating the lengths and weights on each side of a playground seesaw is a static mathematical model.

Static VV&T Techniques are concerned with accuracy assessment on the basis of characteristics of the static model design and source code. Static techniques do not require computer execution of the model, but mental execution can be used.

Steady-State Model is the one whose behavior in one time period is of the same nature as any other period.

Stochastic Activity is an activity the outcome of which varies randomly.

Storage is the process of placing a certified Simulation Model with its full documentation into an organization-wide repository for reuse.

Supportability is the degree to which the M&S application can be supported.

System is any collection of interacting elements that operate to achieve some goal.

System Boundary is the logical and physical partitioning that defines which elements are included within the system definition and which elements are excluded from the system definition.

System Dynamics M&S is the one which uses a model representing cause-and-effect relationships in terms of causal-loop diagrams, flow diagrams with levels and rates, and equations. The equations are used for simulating system behavior. System Dynamics M&S is typically used in disciplines such as Business, Decision Sciences, Economics, Management, Organizational Sciences, Policy Studies, Social Sciences, and System Sciences.

TCP/IP Transmission Control Protocol / Internet Protocol

Technical Independence implies that the M&S application IV&V / Certification Agent determines, prioritizes, and schedules its own tasks and efforts.

Technology-in-the-loop M& Scan be viewed as Simulation-based Technology Evaluation. A technology (e.g., IP-based wireless network, Unmanned Aircraft System, a Satellite Communication System) can be tried, demonstrated or experimented with under simulated scenarios for role players (e.g., subject matter experts, operators, war fighters) to assess how well the proposed technology fulfills its objectives and desired quality characteristics such as Interoperability. In this case, a given technology typically consists of hardware, software, and human operators. Technology-in-the-loop M&S is a cost-effective method for evaluating a potential technology to determine its readiness level and judge if it is ready for deployment for real-world use. Technology-in-the-loop M&S can also be used as a cost-effective method for evaluating human performance and behavior for a proposed technology.

Testability of a requirement is the degree to which the requirement can easily be tested. A testable requirement is the one that is specified in such a way that pass/fail or assessment criteria can be derived from its specification.

Testing is the process of designing a test, specifying test conditions and data, and determining a procedure to follow for the purpose of judging transformational accuracy (verity) and/or representational/behavioral accuracy (validity). Testing is conducted to perform either verification and/or validation.

Time Flow Mechanism is that portion of a simulation that advances time in the simulation, and provides synchronization of the various parts of the simulation.

Traceability of requirements is the degree to which the requirements related to a particular requirement can easily be found. Requirements should be specified in such a way that related requirements are cross-referenced. When it is necessary to change a requirement, those requirements affected by the changed requirement should be easily identified by using the cross-references.

Trace-Driven Simulation is the one which uses the actual input data traced during the operation of the real system so as to drive the model.

Transient Model is the one whose behavior changes with respect to time.

Turing Test is based on the subject matter expert (SME) knowledge about the system under study. The SMEs are presented with two sets of output data obtained, one from the model and one from the system, under the same input conditions. Without identifying which one is which, the SMEs are asked to differentiate between the two. If they succeed, they are asked how they were able to do it. Their response provides valuable feedback for correcting model representation. If they cannot differentiate, our confidence in model validity is increased.

Type I Error is the error of rejecting the credibility of a M/S when in fact the M/S is sufficiently credible.

Type II Error is the error of accepting the credibility of a M/S when in fact the M/S is not sufficiently credible.

Type III Error is the error of solving the wrong problem. It is committed when the formulated problem does not completely contain the actual problem.

UDDI - Universal Description, Discovery and Integration, a web-based distributed directory that enables listing of web services and discovering each other, similar to a traditional phone book's yellow and white pages.

UML - Unified Modeling Language

Unambiguity of a requirement specification is the degree to which the requirement specification can only be interpreted one way.

Understandability of a requirement specification is the degree to which the meaning of the requirement specification is easily comprehended by all of its readers.

Unstable Model is the one which may or may not come back to its initial condition after being disturbed.

Usability is the degree to which the M&S application can easily be employed for its intended use.

Use Case specifies the behavior of a model or a part of a model and is a description of a set of sequences of actions, including variants, that a system performs to yield an observable result of value to an actor. A use case carries out some tangible amount of work.

Validity is the degree of behavioral or representational accuracy.

Variables (Attributes) in the Object-Oriented Paradigm: Characteristics (attributes) of an object are represented by variables. Typically three kinds of variables exist: class variables, instance variables, and local variables.

Class Variables are attributes of a class and are declared in the class for use by the methods of that class and its subclasses and by the objects instantiated from that class and its subclasses.

Instance Variables, declared in a class, are used by the instance methods of that class and are created for each object instantiated as belonging to that class or any of its subclasses, i.e., for each instance of a class, and hence the designator "instance".

Local Variables are declared within a method for use only during the execution of that method. On completion of a method, all local variable values are lost.

Example variables can have the following data types: boolean, character, class reference, object reference, integer number, real number, enumeration.

Verification and Validation (V&V) The terms Verification and Validation (V&V) are consistently defined for whatever entity they are applied to. Let X be that entity such as model, simulation, software, data, or a life cycle artifact (work product) such as requirements specification, conceptual model, design specification, or executable submodel. Then, V&V can be defined generically as follows:

X Verification deals with the assessment of transformational accuracy of the X and addresses the question of "Are we creating the X right?" X Validation deals with the assessment of behavioral or representational accuracy of the X and addresses the question of "Are we creating the right X?"

For whatever entity to be subjected to V&V, substitute the entity name in place of X above, the definitions will hold.

Verity is the degree of transformational accuracy.

Virtual Reality is the use of modeling and simulation to enable a person to interact with a three-dimensional visual representation of a real or imaginary system in an immersive, multi-sensory, and interactive manner. The user wears goggles, headsets, gloves, or body suits to interact with the simulation. The motion sensors pick up the user's movements and adjust his or her view and action accordingly during the interaction, usually in real-time. Virtual Reality is typically used in disciplines such as Architecture, Computer-aided Design and Manufacturing, Education, Entertainment (Movies, Video Games), Human-Computer Interaction, Medical Science, Real Estate, and Training.

VV&T - Verification, Validation, and Testing

WSDL - Web Services Description Language, an XML-formatted language used to describe a Web service's capabilities.

XHTML - Extensible HTML

XML - Extensible Markup Language

XSLT - Extensible Style sheet Language Transformation